SAINT PATRICK'S PURGATORY

Original woodcut in three colours by Eugen Lang, Basel, Switzerland.
Limited edition.

Joseph McGuinness

Saint Patrick's Purgatory
Lough Derg

the columba press

First published in 2000 by
the columba press
55A Spruce Avenue, Stillorgan Industrial Park,
Blackrock, Co Dublin

Cover by Eyecon Design Consultants
Origination by The Columba Press
Printed in Ireland by Colour Books Ltd, Dublin

ISBN 1 85607 295 9

Acknowledgements
The map on p 13 and the woodcut on p 33 are by permission of
the National Library of Ireland. The photographs on pp 47, 53,
55, 57, 59, 64, 67, 69, 71, 73 are by Liam Blake. The photographs
on pp 11, 46, 51 are by Anne Cassidy. All other illustrations are
supplied by Lough Derg.

Contents

Preface

St Patrick's Purgatory, Lough Derg, survives today as a living remnant of the early Irish church, spanning some fifteen centuries of native tenacity, and witness meanwhile to European fame, puritan persecution and Catholic revival. In the current phase of its long story, the pivotal event has been the Second Vatican Council of the 1960s, with its comprehensive vision for church reform and renewal. A most important decision of the council was to return to the original sources of the faith. This meant, in particular, a fresh cultivation of the scriptures in the light of modern scholarship. It also meant presenting church history and teaching in ways that get to the essentials and speak more clearly and more credibly to the men and women of today. It meant ecumenism. It meant an examination by religious orders of their original radical charisms. Those involved in this work soon became aware of the enormity of the task, of the need for slow and patient exploration over many decades, of the struggle to avoid being misunderstood by the general faithful.

I see Father Joseph McGuinness's book in this context of the renewal inspired by the council. People of my generation remember well the excitement of the late sixties when the impact of the council began to filter through to the Irish church. In those days, during the summer months, I used to help out on Lough Derg. The island was, as it has always been, a microcosm of the Irish church in concentrated form. There was little or no initial appetite for renewal. Most of the pilgrims were happy with the old ways and certainly wanted none of the essentials changed. But equally, when it was pointed out to them, they saw the need to keep in line with the universal church, to read the signs of the times. As in the church at large, Lough Derg was ripe for renewal, with all the upsets and risks involved.

The renewal envisaged by the council is evident today in all the key areas of the pilgrimage. There is profound respect for the unchanged core exercises of fasting, station prayers and vigil, all of which have a solid basis in scripture. The revised Rite of Penance has been carefully adapted to the special circumstances of the island. The rich symbolism of the pilgrimage as a whole is kept before pilgrims in order to clarify their vision of Christian living. The struggle to cope with the physical demands of Lough Derg is not seen as an end in itself, its purpose, rather, is to address the deeper conflict in every believer between body and spirit, between natural human instinct and Christian conscience. The serenity of mind, the message of hope and trust in the love and goodness of God, the purging of guilt and fear, all these fruits of Lough Derg are in the end gratuitous and are never in the strict sense earned as of right.

A welcome development on Lough Derg has been the new policy of outreach to the world at large, mainly by way of mass media and the provision of a fulltime office. This is more than about giving pilgrims a better service or about giving the pilgrimage publicity, however important these functions are. I see it as identifying Lough Derg formally with the church's universal mission of reconciliation in a divided society, while remaining at all times part of that society. Pilgrims are encouraged to see themselves as sharing in this mission, but not merely as a random group of individulals who happen to belong to the same church. Their religion is always personal, but not just a private affair. They enter enthusiastically into the island community as a sign of their willingness to play a fuller part in the wider world outside. Of all the areas that call for a new kind of witness on Lough Derg, sensitive and realistic concern for the healing and liberating work of the church in society is the most challenging and the most significant in the long run.

In recent years, the eucharistic liturgy on Lough Derg has come to reflect a keener sense of belonging to the church as a community. The Mass on the evening of the first day brings all pilgrims together for the first time. The formal greeting at the beginning invites the pilgrims to see themselves as a community of believers and to strive for that greater community which we call the kingdom of God. While this is a feature of every Mass, it is seldom so thoroughly prepared for as on the evening of the first day on Lough Derg. Similarly, the eucharist on the morning of the third day has all the joy and excitement of the first witnesses of the resurrection. There is a new life and warmth in our respect for each other, brought about through our sharing in the exercises and following a good night's sleep.

Pilgrims are more conscious these days of the spiritual atmosphere of the island. Lough Derg began, probably in the sixth century, as a monastic retreat, a place of prayer and contemplation away from social and commercial life. It was a *díseart,* an Irish version of the biblical desert, the wilderness of the prophet Isaiah and John the Baptist. In today's noisy and turbulent world, pilgrims appreciate a haven of peace, a remote corner where the discomfort of physical discipline is more than compensated for by getting away from the stress of modern-day living. They talk about the therapy of shedding unnecessary baggage, of recovering a simple rhythm of life, of getting back to the essential human need to praise God, to give thanks, to seek direction. The extensive additions to the buildings and the ground space of the island in the late 1980s have added immeasurably to the potential for personal space and quiet. To make better use of these improved facilities, while protecting the traditional three-day pilgrimage season from June to August, special one-day retreats have been introduced during the months of May and September. This enables the island to cater for the first time for those who are handicapped by age and disability.

The author of this volume is an experienced priest-teacher who also ministers on Lough Derg. With these credentials he is ideally equipped to give us a well-informed and up-to-date survey of a place that is altogether unique in the world. He writes expressly for the general reader. May I commend his readable

account to those who know Lough Derg already and to those
who wish to know more about it.

✠ *Joseph Duffy*
Bishop of Clogher
17 March 2000

CHAPTER ONE

Origins and Development of the Pilgrimage

The Name

The placenames of Ireland provide ample opportunities for confusion, especially for the non-native. There are many examples of the same placename appearing two, three or more times in locations far distant from one another. So it is that, even in recent times, the existence of two Lough Dergs, one on the Shannon river, the other in Co Donegal, has caused confusion to more than one prospective pilgrim. The root of this problem is the anglicisation of old Irish names, which has often caused names which might have had very different Irish roots to be transcribed in identical ways in their English forms. This has also resulted in confusion over the original Irish form of the name and hence its origin and meaning. For many years it was assumed that the name of Lough Derg in Donegal derived from the Irish *Loch Dearg* (the Red Lake). In several accounts written in the Middle Ages, the origin of the name is ascribed to the slaying by St Patrick of a monster, whose blood turned the waters of the lake red. One account in particular tells of St Patrick fighting with the devil's mother, who then escaped to Lough Derg only to be pursued by the saint and eventually killed. More recently it has been suggested that the correct origin of the name is the word *Derc* (or in some cases *Gercc*) which means a pit or a cave. As we shall see, this interpretation fits in well with what we know of the origins of the Lough Derg pilgrimage.

The Island

The pilgrimage today is centred on the tiny island called Station Island. The earliest Christian settlement was, however, founded on Saints' Island, a much larger island, lying about two miles northwest of Station Island. Here in the fifth century a monastic community was set up. There is very little by way of archaeological or documentary evidence about the precise origins of the monastery of Lough Derg, although St Patrick was traditionally believed to have been its founder. This tradition only became firmly established in the twelfth century and hard evidence to associate the saint directly with the lake is practically non-existent. There is some evidence to suggest that St Patrick travelled in the vicinity of Lough Derg. It is quite possible that he may have been attracted by the remoteness of the place to escape the cares of his mission and spend some time in prayer in the bleak countryside which surrounds the lake.

The harsh beauty of lake and landscape may very well have been an important factor in the decision of the early Celtic monks to create a community on what came to be known as Saints' Island. It is worth noting also that Celtic pagan cults seem to have been very strong in the area between Lough Derg and Lough Erne. We know that many of the most significant pagan sites of worship in Ireland were taken over and christianised by the early missionaries. Such places included mountains, woods, wells and other natural features sacred to the Celtic gods. Local placenames strongly suggest that this process took place in the case of Lough Derg and the surrounding area. For centuries the summit of one of the hills to the south of the lake has been known as Saint Davog's Chair. Similarly, the name of Saint Brigid's Chair has been applied to a large rock on the shore of the lake. As recently as the nineteenth century, pilgrims who had completed their stations and were travelling on foot from Lough Derg continued the practice of stopping at a spring, known as the Holy Well of Cullion. Here each one would leave a rounded pebble as a votive gift. This well is located southeast of the lake not far from Drumawark hill where until 1880 stood a cross which directed pilgrims on the final part of their journey to the island. From the summit of this hill it is possible to view from Lough Derg across to Lough Erne, taking in the ancient

St Brigid's Chair

pagan sites of Boa Island and, in the distance, the ruins of the famous monastery of Devenish.

The Early Monastery
The first abbot of the monastery of Lough Derg is reckoned to have been St Davog, supposedly a disciple of St Patrick. Davog is also the name of another saintly abbot of Lough Derg who lived in the seventh century. The name is preserved locally to this day both in the aforementioned St Davog's Chair and the neighbouring Seadavog mountain. We know very little of the life or work of either of these saints and indeed our knowledge of the early history of the Celtic monastic community on Lough Derg is very limited. Old Irish writings such as the *Annals of Ulster* and the *Annals of the Four Masters* make a few passing references to the monastery. We are told that in 721 Cillene of *Locha Gercc* died, possibly a reference to one of the early abbots of

Lough Derg. The famous round tower on the monastic island of Devenish on Lough Erne reminds us of the vulnerability of the Irish monasteries to plundering raids. It is unlikely that the monastery on Lough Derg escaped the attentions of the Vikings who, according to the *Annals of the Four Masters*, destroyed all the churches of Lough Erne in 836. The *Annals* also refer to the plundering of Lough Derg by Irish chieftains in 1070 and again in 1111.

Coping with the constant threat of raids by both native and foreign marauders was only one harsh reality in the lives of the monks. As in the other famous monasteries of the Celtic church, such as Clonmacnoise and Glendalough, the monks of Lough Derg daily endured a severe and frugal existence, their lives revolving around prayer and work. Not content with the austerity of daily life in the monastery, many monks elected to submit themselves to the harshest of penances. Most of the monasteries had associated with them special places of retreat where individual monks could go to spend long periods in prayer and fasting. These places were usually not far from the monasteries themselves, although separated from them by barriers of both a natural and a mental kind. By the sixth century such a retreat had been established by the monks of Saints' Island. The location they chose was the island now known as Station Island. Here they eventually constructed small bee-hive cells, which provided meagre shelter for those who opted to spend lengthy periods fasting, reciting long litanies of prayer and undertaking harsh physical penances. It is this belief in the heroism of self-mortification that leaves the deepest impression upon us today and which formed the character of the Lough Derg pilgrimage.

The Early Pilgrimages

For Lough Derg the twelfth century was the century of transformation. We do not know for certain when Lough Derg first became a centre of pilgrimage. What we do know is that by the end of the twelfth century the island was well on its way to becoming one of the most renowned places of pilgrimage in the Christian world. The rapid rise of Saint Patrick's Purgatory to a

An early map of Ireland featuring St Patrick's Purgatory very prominently. By permission of the National Library of Ireland.

position of fame rivalling any of the great medieval shrines seems to have depended on several factors. Chief among these was the great change that began in the Irish church in the middle of the twelfth century.

Christianity had flourished in Ireland since the fifth century, and the island had been fortunate in escaping the ravages of the barbarian invasions which had finally destroyed the Roman Empire. It was this relative peace which had allowed Ireland to become, in truth, the Island of Saints and Scholars. It had also, however, had the effect of isolating the Irish church from the

Christian communities on the continent, with the result that the practice of religion in Ireland developed in uniquely characteristic ways. These included an organisational structure based on the Celtic monasteries as centres of ecclesiastical power, rather than the diocesan system that came to prevail on the continent. Although St Patrick had founded churches and placed them in the care of bishops, as Christianity consolidated and developed it was increasingly the monasteries and their abbots which exercised the real power in the Irish church. In the twelfth century, as the Church of Rome neared the apogee of its spiritual and temporal influence in Europe, this all began to change. The continental church, which had been so enriched by the labours of Celtic missionaries such as Columbanus, Feargal and Killian, began to exert its own influence on the church in Ireland. One of the chief architects of this reformation was the great Archbishop of Armagh, St Malachy. It was Malachy who was responsible for the introduction into the north of Ireland of, among others, the Augustinian Order of Canons Regular, an event of momentous significance for Lough Derg. The Augustinians established an abbey at Armagh, dedicated to Saints Peter and Paul, in the 1140s. At about the same time, canons from this abbey were installed on Saints' Island and took over the running of the monastery there. They were subject to the authority of a Prior who was himself subordinate to the abbot of the monastery in Armagh. It is worth noting that the priest in charge of the pilgrimage, although now a diocesan priest, is still known as the Prior of Lough Derg.

The introduction of continental religious orders such as the Augustinians and the Cistercians was only a part of the reform of the Irish church which began to take place at this time. Already at the Synod of Rathbreasail (1111) and later at the Synod of Kells (1152), the Irish dioceses had been established and their boundaries fixed, much as we know them today. Power in the church shifted markedly away from the old Celtic monastic foundations and was secured in the hands of the new diocesan bishops. In the northern kingdom of Airghialla, in which Lough Derg was situated, these new reforms were quickly established. An obituary of Donnchadh O Cearbhaill, King of Airghialla (1168), reads: 'A prayer for Donnchadh O Cearbhaill. It is he who renewed the church in the land of Airghialla, who made a regular bishopric, who brought the church under episcopal control. It is in his time that tithes were taken, churches and bell-towers made, monasteries of monks and canons and nuns renewed.' One of these monasteries was almost certainly the monastery on Saints' Island.

The arrival of the Augustinians did not mean the immediate demise of the Celtic monastic way of life. We know that the Augustinians who were established at the neighbouring monastery on Devenish Island on Lough Erne continued to co-exist with a community of Celtic monks or culdees up to the time of the seventeenth century plantation. Just as newly-arrived Christianity had successfully absorbed aspects of the pre-existent pagan culture, so the new monastic orders assimilated certain aspects of the old Celtic monastic tradition.

It is with the coming of the Augustinians to Lough Derg that we first find hard evidence of a pilgrimage dedicated to St Patrick and reputedly founded by him. This is at least in part because the Irish church was now more integrated into the fabric of Roman Christendom. The international nature of religious orders such as the Augustinians supported easier communications, as well as a natural tendency to promote as widely as possible those shrines and pilgrimages in their care. It is at this time too that the earliest written accounts of the pilgrimage appear. The first and most famous of these is the story of the pilgrimage of the Knight Owein. This account became extremely popular, not only in Ireland and Britain, but also throughout Europe. There are some one hundred and fifty copies of the original Latin text still to be found in libraries all over the continent as well as numerous translations. The tale of Knight Owein not only spread the fame of St Patrick's Purgatory far and wide, but it was also an important influence on the European imagination of the later Middle Ages.

The story was written down in 1184 by a Cistercian monk of the abbey of Saltrey in Huntingdonshire, England. The monk identifies himself simply by the initial H, and records that the story came to him from another monk by the name of Gilbert. This Gilbert had spent some time in Ireland between the years 1148 and 1150, when he had been involved in the founding of a monastery. The local king assigned to him a knight called Owein, to act as an interpreter. It was during their time working together that Owein recounted his experiences to Gilbert. Brother H of Saltrey did not hear the story until some thirty years later and recorded it under the title *Tractatus de Purgatorio Sancti Patricii* (Treatise on St Patrick's Purgatory). We shall have cause to refer later to some of the details described in the *Tractatus* insofar as they illuminate our understanding of the development of the exercises of the pilgrimage, but it will suffice here to give just a very brief outline of the document.

Owein's tale describes how he came to Lough Derg and there experienced a journey into the next world. His account is prefaced by a long introduction in which H discusses the realities of the afterlife. The mysterious world beyond death was a source of endless fascination for the people of the Middle Ages in general, and medieval theologians in particular. In his introduction, H of Saltrey shows himself to be no less fascinated than his contemporaries:

> We know that many have often asked in what manner the souls leave the body, where do they go, what do they find, what do they perceive and what do they suffer. Because these things have been concealed from us, it is better to fear them than to inquire about them.

It is hardly surprising that Owein's account should have become so popular, since it purports to reveal some of the answers to these questions, nor that the place in which these revelations were made should acquire such vast renown.

It is important to note, however, that Owein's motive for travelling to Lough Derg was not the expectation of some extraordinary vision, but rather the same motive that has inspired pilgrims to this very day. The knight, having confessed his sins to the local bishop, was so moved by remorse that he responded to the bishop's admonition as follows:

> Since you declare that I have so greatly offended my Creator, I will take on a penance more arduous than any penance. For in order to be worthy of receiving the remission of my sins, I will, with your encouragement, enter Saint Patrick's Purgatory.

In spite of the bishop's warnings of the dangers involved, Owein was determined to go. Eventually the bishop gave him permission and sent him off to the island with a letter to the prior, recommending that he be allowed to enter the purgatory.

When he arrived at Lough Derg, Owein went to the monastery on Saints' Island. On hearing his request the prior also strenuously discouraged him, warning him that others before him had entered the purgatory, never to return. Owein nevertheless insisted and so the prior admitted him to the church, where he spent fifteen days in prayer and fasting. At the end of this period the knight was taken to the Purgatory of St Patrick. Here he was admitted through a door into a dark cavern or pit. Having continued through the dark for some time, he eventually saw light ahead and emerged into a large field. In the centre of the field was a large and beautifully built hall. On entering the hall he was soon met by fifteen men dressed in white, who proved to be messengers from God. They warned him that he would be assaulted by demons, who would try to persuade him to turn back and leave the place. Owein remained steadfast. No sooner had these angels disappeared than the demons appeared. In spite of their threats of torture Owein refused to retreat. The demons at once seized him and began to subject him to the first of ten ordeals. This involved dragging him with iron hooks backwards and forwards through a blazing fire. At first the pain was unbearable, but when Owein called on the name of Jesus the fire instantly disappeared. The same pattern held for the remaining nine torments. In each case Owein was released by invoking the name of the Saviour. It is worth noting that these torments were also being inflicted on other human beings 'of both sexes and all ages'. These were the souls of the dead, unable to avail of the prayer which had saved the knight.

The same prayer helped Owein to escape from the devils and enter into a beautiful and fertile land filled with a multitude of people. There were choirs singing and everyone was filled with joy. Here he was met by two archbishops, who explained to him that the place through which he had journeyed was the place in which the souls of the dead were purified through torment. Eventually they would be released into the earthly paradise which he now saw. From there they would finally ascend to the paradise of heaven. Eventually Owein had to leave this paradise and return to earth by the way he came. This time the demons fled before him, and he safely reached the door by which he had entered, to be greeted joyfully by the prior. Returning to the church, Owein then spent a further fifteen days in prayer. H of Saltrey then concludes his work with the evidence of other witnesses who have assured him of the reality of this purgatory and the terrible things that had happened there.

The Age of Visions
The extent of the influence of the *Tractatus* is revealed not only by the large number and widespread distribution of copies and translations, but also by the allusions to its story which are to be found in the literature and art of the later Middle Ages. Its influence on writers such as Marie de France and Dante has often been cited. An interesting aspect of this process is the way in which St Patrick came to be closely associated with the realm of purgatory and the souls of the dead. One striking example can be seen in the fresco recovered in 1974 in a convent at Todi in northern Italy. The fresco was painted in 1346 but whitewashed over about 1600. It depicts a large cavern in which the souls of the dead are tormented in a variety of ways. There are seven holes in the walls, each one labelled with the name of one of the seven deadly sins. Through these openings we can see the particular punishments which each group of souls endures. Most significantly, above the cavern is a chimney through which the fires are stoked by none other than St Patrick himself. We can see

that this cavern is meant to represent purgatory, since the purified souls emerge from it to be greeted by Our Lady and St Philip Benizi before being ushered by St Peter into the kingdom of heaven.

We are well aware today of the appetite which people have for signs and wonders, visions and apparitions. In the middle ages such things exerted an even more powerful fascination. It is certainly true that pilgrims of those times were drawn to Lough Derg for the same motive of repentance as the Knight Owein. St Patrick's Purgatory was considered, then as now, to be a place which could provide penance to match any sin. But it is also true that pilgrims from all over Europe were drawn to the island by its reputation as a gateway to the next world. As a result, the pilgrimage gave rise to a rich tradition of literature concerning the visions which were widely believed to be experienced there. We have accounts of such visions from pilgrims throughout the fourteenth and fifteenth centuries. Their stories are usually similar in outline to that of the Knight Owein, but they are often highly elaborate in structure and detail.

The terrors and tortures of purgatory become increasingly ingenious and graphic. The Hungarian pilgrim George of Grissaphan, who came to Lough Derg in 1353, found himself tempted by the devil who disguised himself as a ravishingly beautiful woman. George found the strength to resist when he caught sight of the lady's feet, one of which belonged to a cow, the other to a horse. In 1397 the island was visited by Ramon de Perellos, a Catalan. Among the many terrors of his vision, Ramon was shown many of his friends and relatives being cruelly tortured for their sins. William of Stranton, an English pilgrim about 1406, describes how in his vision he was shown the variety of punishments prescribed for specific sins. Robbers were to be seen being attacked by their stolen goods while people who had revelled or indulged themselves in taverns on holy days were being stuffed like turkeys with filth.

It was inevitable that some pilgrims, anticipating these horrors with a somewhat delicious dread, should leave the island disappointed. One of these was a certain Dutch monk from the town of Eymstadt. Perhaps the fact that he had no money to pay to the bishop or the prior was to blame. In any case, having been lowered into a pit to spend the night, he waited in fear and trembling for the expected vision. He waited in vain: no demons, no torments, no vision. When he was retrieved the following morning, the monk was more angry than frightened. So angry was he that he had a complaint lodged with the Pope. His protests seem to have been successful. *The Annals of Ulster* record for 1497:

> The Cave of the Purgatory of St Patrick on Loch Gearg was broken this year by the Guardian of Donegal and by the representatives of the Bishop in the Deanery of Lough Erne by authorisation of the Pope about the feast of St Patrick of this year: it being understood by everyone in general from the history of the knight and other old books that this was not the Purgatory Patrick got from God although they were, everyone, visiting it.'

Whatever may have happened to this cave, it is clear that the pilgrimage itself was hardly interrupted. *The Annals of Ulster* go on to record the visit of a French pilgrim in 1516, while no less a personage than the Papal Nuncio to Henry VIII visited the island in the following year. However it is noticeable that from about this time the stories of journeys to the next world and the fantastic visions of purgatory and paradise begin to disappear. However, the decline of the visionary tradition allowed the older and more fundamental penitential nature of the pilgrimage to predominate.

Turbulent Times

In this sense it seemed that the pilgrimage was to proceed just as before. The coming of the Reformation at first had little impact on the monastery of Lough Derg. The continuing ascendancy of the Gaelic chieftains, particularly in the north of Ireland, meant that measures such as the Dissolution of the Monasteries by Henry VIII caused no disruption to the traditional religious practice of the area. From the early Middle Ages the sanctuary, or Termon, of Lough Derg, although the property of the church, had formed part of the lands which were under the civil rule of the local clan, the MacGraths. Several of the MacGrath clan had held the office of Prior of Lough Derg. The monastery and pilgrimage enjoyed the protection of the local chieftain, while the rights of the church were respected. Political developments in the sixteenth century were to put an end to this arrangement and bring about a long period of conflict and uncertainty in the history of the pilgrimage.

It was during these times that the English Crown made its final and successful effort to subdue the northern part of Ireland. The local chieftains were able to retain their land by submitting to the authority of the monarch and renouncing the Catholic religion. Records show that in 1596 the lands of Termon MacGrath were surrendered by Donnchadh MacGrath to Queen Elizabeth I. The lands were immediately regranted to him and his heirs. The turmoil in Ireland had already led to the abandonment of the monastery on Saints' Island by the Augustinians. A survey of 1603 reported that the 'priory now is very much on the decay, and has these many years past been totally abandoned and dissolved'. The monastery was never to be rebuilt, and hardly a trace of it can be seen today. Nevertheless some of the monks remained to oversee the pilgrimage, which continued on Station Island.

As the English government consolidated its grip on the country, however, the pilgrimage itself came under direct attack. In the eyes of the Reformers, Lough Derg represented a particularly repellent example of Catholic superstition, a view reinforced by the many legends and visions associated with the place. Given the religious climate of the time, it is hardly surprising that, in 1632, orders were given by the Lords Justices for the destruction of St Patrick's Purgatory. These orders were carried out under the direction of the Anglican Bishop of Clogher, James Spottiswoode. The monks were driven from the island. The cave, penitential beds and all other buildings were completely levelled. This destruction is one of the main reasons why there are so few relics of the earlier centuries of the pilgrimage to be seen on the island today. The reaction of the local people is apparent from the following extract taken from the report which the bishop wrote to Dr Ussher, the Protestant Archbishop of Armagh:

> The country people expected that St Patrick would have wrought some miracles; but thanks be to God none of my company received any other harm than the bad waves, broken cawsies, and the dangers of going in a little boat: yet one comfort is, that we effected that for which we came hither, which was more than was expected could be done in so short a time, which hath wonderfully displeased them who were bewitched with these fooleries.

Dr Spottiswoode's satisfaction was misplaced. We are told that even while access to the island was denied, people still came to the lake to pray and to perform the pilgrimage exercises of fast and vigil as best they could. It is said that while they prayed at the lake shore they often extended their hands towards the island. This longing to return was quickly fulfilled. It was impossible for the authorities to keep effective watch over the lake and within a few years pilgrims had restarted the pilgrimage on Station Island. They did their best to retrieve, even from the lake bed, any old stones and relics which were salvageable. The penitential beds were reconstructed, as was the cave and other very basic buildings. Since the departure of the Augustinians, the care of the pilgrims had been taken over by the Franciscan Order. For the next one hundred and fifty years, the Franciscans were to sustain the pilgrimage, often at great risk to themselves. Although the severity of the Penal laws was intermittent, it was not until the time as prior of Fr Anthony O'Doherty in 1763 that the friars felt sufficiently secure to establish a residence on the island.

Throughout the rest of the seventeenth century and the first half of the eighteenth, the pattern of suppression continued. Orders would be given, laws enacted, but the pilgrimage did not disappear. That it continued to thrive is shown by an Act of

Queen Anne which in 1704 complained that 'the superstitions of Popery are greatly increased and upheld by the pretended sanctity of places, especially a place called St Patrick's Purgatory in the County of Donegal …' The Act goes on to forbid any kind of assembly at Lough Derg and prescribes that offenders should be fined ten shillings. If the fine was not paid, the offender was to be whipped in public. Although not repealed until 1871, neither this nor any other official measure seems to have had any serious effect on the continuity of the pilgrimage, as many accounts of the period confirm. The vehemence of the attacks on the pilgrimage by Protestant writers demonstrates clearly the power of its endurance. In this connection it is worth noting the later contribution of the famous Tyrone writer, William Carleton. Carleton came to Lough Derg as a pilgrim in 1820. Shortly afterwards he published an essay in *The Christian Examiner and Church of Ireland Magazine* which launched his literary career. Entitled 'The Lough Derg Pilgrim', the article ridiculed the pilgrimage. It has been argued since that the article was heavily edited by the journal's editor, the Rev Caesar Otway. Whatever the truth of this, it remains surprising that Carleton, who was born a Catholic and once aspired to the priesthood, should have allowed this kind of piece to be published. By this time, however, the worst days of persecution and suppression were over. As the eighteenth century drew to a close, the pilgrimage was already moving into its modern phase.

Renewal
The first real sign of renewal appeared in 1763 with the building of a small church on the island. This was the church of the Blessed Virgin Mary of the Angels, erected by the Franciscan prior of the time, Father Anthony O'Doherty. This was followed in 1780 by the opening of another, larger church dedicated to St Patrick. This replaced the famous cave, which had been closed up. Both churches were to be rebuilt and renovated on several occasions. The present St Mary's church dates from 1870, while the old church of St Patrick has been replaced by the present Basilica. A dedication stone from the old St Mary's church can

The interior of St Mary's Church

still be seen, set into the wall of the Basilica, along with other old inscribed stones. The new security enjoyed by the pilgrimage is also demonstrated by the fact that the building of the churches was accompanied by the construction of accommodation for the priests who worked on the island.

Throughout the nineteenth and twentieth centuries the process of enlarging and improving the facilities for pilgrims to the island has continued. The appearance of the island today is therefore the product of the efforts of the last two hundred years or so. The men's hostel dates originally from 1880, although the interior was extensively renovated in 1995. The next major project was the building of the women's hostel, completed in 1912. This building, in concrete rather than stone, failed to stand the test of time. In the 1980s it was decided to provide completely new accommodation for female pilgrims. The new hostel building, opened in 1988, not only provides accommodation but also houses the island laundry as well as the pilgrims' dining room.

The interior of St Patrick's Church

In 1931 the new St Patrick's church, soon to be constituted as a Basilica, was consecrated. The uniqueness of this building and the role it plays in the pilgrimage will be discussed in a later chapter. It is worth noting here that this massive building is built almost entirely on concrete piles sunk into the bed of the lake. Indeed hardly any of the buildings now to be seen on the island are in fact built entirely on the island itself. Most, including the staff house constructed in 1961, are built on land reclaimed from the lake. The impression given is that the island is much larger than a mere acre of land.

The increase in building activity was galvanised by the new-found freedom of the Catholic faith in the nineteenth century. This was reflected in the increase in the number of pilgrims to Lough Derg, a trend which demanded developments not only in the physical arrangements on the island, but also in the administration of the pilgrimage. Already in the late 1700s the Franciscans had found themselves unable to continue as overseers of the pilgrimage. Lack of numbers in the Order resulted in their withdrawal in favour of the more securely established diocesan clergy. From about 1780 onwards the Prior of Lough Derg has been appointed by the Bishop of Clogher and the island has been staffed by priests of the diocese. Accurate records of the numbers of pilgrims to Lough Derg are only available from 1866. For the years previous to this we have to rely on the reported impressions of individual pilgrims and priests. Allowing for the fact that these tend to be overestimated (a small island can appear crowded even when a relatively small number of people are present), it still seems reasonable to accept that there was a very marked increase in the numbers of pilgrims in the wake of Catholic Emancipation. This increase was drastically halted by the Famine, after which the yearly total of pilgrims settled at around two to three thousand. The twentieth century has seen the most dramatic surge in pilgrim numbers, particularly once the disruptions of the early 1920s had passed. The peak was reached in 1953 with a total of 34,645 pilgrims. Since then numbers have fluctuated, although always remaining well into five figures. Many of these modern-day pilgrims are from overseas, demonstrating an international interest in Lough Derg which recalls its medieval fame.

What is it about this remarkable pilgrimage which has allowed it not just to survive but to grow, in spite of the many difficulties it has faced? Why does Lough Derg continue to exercise such a strong fascination, even attraction, in the late twentieth century? The answer to both these questions lies in the nature of the pilgrimage itself. Those elements of the pilgrimage which give it its unique and enduring quality will be the subjects of the next chapters.

Bell-tower and beds, showing 'cabins' in the background.
These cabins (pilgrim accomodation by families who 'owned' houses
on the island) were demolished in 1953.

CHAPTER TWO

The Vigil

The practice of spending long periods in prayer and meditation is common to many religions. In the Christian tradition it may be traced to the example of Christ himself. The gospels tell us of various occasions when Jesus sought solitude in order to pray. Perhaps the prototype for the Lough Derg vigil may be found in the garden of Gethsemane, where Our Lord spent the night in prayer before his arrest. Christ's command to his disciples on that occasion to stay awake and to pray has drawn a response from devout Christians ever since. Indeed the high-point of the liturgy of the church is the great Vigil of Easter, when Christians gather to spend at least part of the night in joyful praise of the Risen Lord.

Vigil in the Celtic church
We know that keeping vigil was a common practice in the Celtic church. In those times it was not just a part of the common liturgical celebration but also an accepted form of penance. In one of the old Irish *Penitentials*, which lists the appropriate penances for various sins, a recommended penance is to spend the night 'in cold churches or remote cells while keeping vigil and praying without respite, without leave to sit or lie down or sleep – as though one were at the very gates of hell – unless a little weariness chance to occur between two cycles of prayer, when one may sit'. This is a description with which any pilgrim to Lough Derg will very easily identify.

From the earliest records of the Lough Derg pilgrimage until the present day, the vigil has been considered the central and most important of the penitential exercises. For most pilgrims it remains the most difficult. The simple task of staying awake continuously for twenty-four hours is not easy at the best of times. When combined with the rigours of the fast and the station prayers, it presents a daunting challenge. That the twenty-four hour vigil has always been considered the real test of the pilgrimage is clear from the earliest detailed account, the *Tractatus* of H of Saltrey. This account also highlights a unique aspect of the vigil. This is its close association with the cave or pit which existed on the island from earlier times. For centuries this cave was the central focus of the pilgrimage. Although it has now disappeared, the practices associated with it can still be traced in the modern pilgrimage. It is therefore worthwhile to take a brief look at its origins and significance.

The Origins of the Cave

An account of the cave's origins is given in the *Tractatus*. This story seems to be based on older legends, mixed together with details designed to enhance the prestige of the Augustinians. According to the *Tractatus*, the cave (or pit) was first revealed to St Patrick by Christ himself. While Patrick was trying to spread the gospel in Ireland, the people proved to be somewhat stubborn. In spite of his preaching and miracles, they refused to be converted unless at least one of them could see for himself the punishments of the wicked and the rewards of the good. Then they could be sure that these were not empty promises. In response, Patrick dedicated himself to a regime of prayer, fasting and vigils on the people's behalf. It was then that the Lord Jesus Christ appeared to him, presenting him with a book of the gospels and a staff. The account continues:

> So the Lord took Saint Patrick to a deserted place. There he showed to him a round pit, dark inside, and said to him that whoever, being truly repentant and armed with true faith, would enter this pit and remain for the duration of one day and one night, would be purged of all the sins of his life. Moreover, while going through it, he would see not only the torments of the wicked, but also, if he acted constantly according to the faith, the joys of the blessed ... [Patrick] immediately had a church built in this place and there he

installed canons of the blessed father Augustine who were leading an apostolic life. As for this pit, which is in the grave-yard outside the west wall of the church, he had it enclosed within a wall and doors and had locks added so that nobody would enter by rash audacity and without permission ... And since men were purged of their sins there, this place was called Saint Patrick's Purgatory.'

Whatever the exact origins of this particular cave may have been, the practice of spending long periods of time praying in caves or cells was well established in the early Irish church. These cells were usually located near a monastery. Some resorted to these cells in order to do penance for particular sins. Others, including lay-people, entered them in their later years as a way of retiring from this world and preparing for the next. Many instances are recorded in the old lives of the Irish saints and in chronicles such as the *Annals of the Four Masters,* where these people are described as being 'on pilgrimage'. St Molaise of Devenish, we are told, 'loved to be in a hard prison of stone'. That such a 'hard prison' had been revealed to St Patrick would certainly have added prestige to the cave on Lough Derg. Its standing would have been further enhanced by its connection with the world beyond death.

Although frequently described as a 'cave', the purgatory was almost certainly man-made. The descriptions given in the various accounts of the Middle Ages and afterwards seem to indicate that there was a long pit dug out of the ground and then covered over with walls and a roof. Some of the descriptions are very exaggerated, or come from secondhand accounts. Visionary tales, such as that of the Knight Owein, neglect to give much description of the cave itself, being more concerned to describe the otherworld to which it was merely the entrance. But the picture that emerges of the cave is of a relatively rough construction. Pilgrims of the later Middle Ages describe it as being long and narrow with a turn or corner towards one end. The roof was so low that it was possible to kneel but not to stand. Bishop Spottiswoode, sent to destroy it in 1632, reported that:

Carve's 1666 map of the island

the cave was a poor beggarly hole, made with some stones, laid together with men's hands without any great art; and after covered with earth, such as husbandmen make to keep a few hogs from the rain.

Having been rebuilt, the cave appears on a map of the island published by Thomas Carve in 1666, looking much as the accounts had described it. One of the last descriptions of the cave before its final destruction is that of the Protestant John Richardson in 1727:

It was 22 feet long, 2 feet 1 inch wide, and 3 feet high. It hath a bending within six feet of the far end, where there is a very small window, or spike hole, to let in some light and air to the pilgrims that are shut up in it. There is little or none of it under ground, and it seems never to have been sunk deeper than the rock. It is built of stone and clay, huddled together, covered with broad stones, and all overlaid with earth.

This then was the famous 'cave' which was the home of the
Lough Derg vigil for centuries. It is clear from these descriptions
that the cave could not have accommodated a large number of
pilgrims. As the penal times drew to a close, the crowds of
pilgrims began to swell significantly and it was mainly for this
reason that the cave was finally abandoned and demolished in
1780.

The doctrine of purgatory
With the disappearance of the cave the term 'St Patrick's
Purgatory' came to refer to the island in general, whereas previously it had applied only to the cave itself. The cave had enjoyed
its greatest fame at a time when the doctrine of purgatory was
becoming integrated into the Christian view of the next world.
Visionary accounts such as that of the Knight Owein helped to
establish the notion of purgatory as a place in the afterlife quite
distinct from heaven and hell. The familiar images of agony,
previously invoked as the fate of the damned, were recast and
applied to a place of purification or purging for those who were
destined for heaven but were not yet worthy of their eternal
reward. The visionary tradition not only gave lurid expression
to this view – as the Todi fresco vividly testifies – but also presented the cave as a doorway to that place of passing torment. It
was through his vigil in the cave that the pilgrim gained access
to the domain of purgatory. This association of the cave and the
location of purgatory had all but disappeared by the time the
cave was finally destroyed. By then the period of visions was
long gone.

The account of the monk of Eymstadt is perhaps an indic-
ation of a growing mood of scepticism towards the tales of
otherworldly journeys. Certainly the Papal suppression of the
supposed false cave in 1497, however brief in duration, marks a
watershed between the visionary tradition and the more sombre,
purely penitential pilgrimage which was to emerge subsequently.

Another letter, this time by Donatus McGrath, Prior of Lough
Derg in 1507, shows clearly the shift in emphasis which was taking place in the pilgrimage. This letter gives us some of the earli-

A woodcut of purgatory from a fifteenth-century German manuscript on Lough Derg. National Library of Ireland.

est evidence that the island was becoming officially recognised
as a place of penance. Rather than being the gateway to the actual
realm of purgatory, the cave is now simply an element of the
whole ensemble of penances which constitute the pilgrimage as
we would recognise it today. Donatus commends the bearer of
the letter as a pilgrim who has:

> done all the pilgrimages of the island of the said Purgatory,
> and has stayed in the ditch of the same Saint Patrick for a nat-
> ural day; if he has seen or experienced any punishments or
> torments he did so bodily.

This more sober perception of the pilgrimage, and in particular the vigil, is apparent in an account of a visit to Lough Derg
sent to Rome in 1714 by the then Bishop of Clogher, Hugh
MacMahon. Having described the rigours of the fast and the
Station prayers, the bishop continues:

> On the ninth day, having first made a general confession,
> having expiated all the faults of their life, and being nour-
> ished with the Bread of Life, they enter before twilight a sub-
> terranean pit, which is called the Purgatory, and here they
> remain four and twenty continuous hours, all the time awake
> and engaged in prayer, without any refreshment either of
> food or drink. When the same hour arrives on the following
> day, they go forth and dip their heads thrice in the cold water.
> And thus is completed the pilgrimage, to which idle inventors
> of fables have added so many exaggerations about spectres
> and visions, which never had any existence save in the dis-
> torted imaginations of such storytellers.

One interesting aspect of Bishop MacMahon's account is his
reference to the continuation of a practice whose origins belong
to the old visionary tradition. Several of the visionary accounts
mention that a Requiem Mass was said for the pilgrims before
they entered the cave. Although this was linked by these writers
to the possibility that the pilgrims might not emerge alive from
the terrors of the cave, the bishop imagines it to be a symbol that
the pilgrims were renouncing the comforts of this life 'just as if
they were dead to the world'. This view would certainly accord

with the Celtic Christian notion of the retirement to a cell as being a complete withdrawal from the world. When the bishop suggested changes to the practice, so that on Sundays and feasts the Proper Masses might be said, he says that the Franciscan Fathers 'claimed the authority of immemorial possession and of custom to the contrary, first originated, as tradition says, by Saint Patrick himself; which, being constantly asserted by learned and scrupulous men, has perplexed me'.

The Basilica

After the demolition of the cave the vigil was conducted in the newly built church of St Patrick. This church came to be known as the 'Prison Chapel', a title derived from the old tradition of pilgrims being locked or shut in to the cave. It is also aptly reminiscent of St Molaise's 'hard prison of stone'. The frequent rebuilding and renovation of the Prison Chapel indicate that it was never fully adequate to its purpose. The capacity of the church was only about three hundred people and it was frequently the case that many pilgrims had to spend the night of their vigil in the open air, regardless of the weather. In the early years of this century the decision was taken to demolish the church completely and to replace it with a much larger and grander building. It is worth describing the origins and nature of this modern-day successor to the famous cave.

The original designs for the church were commissioned from Professor W. A. Scott, one of the leading Irish architects of the day. In 1919 Scott was invited to Lough Derg to survey the site of the new church. He spent a night on the island, observing the pilgrimage and absorbing the role which the church on the island played as the main location of the vigil and the centre for liturgical celebrations. In the morning he asked one of the boatmen to take him out on the lake some distance from the island. He was then able to view the island and its buildings from all angles. Returning to the island, he informed the prior that he had his design completed. Within a short space of time, the plans were drawn. Unfortunately the political strife of the early 1920s prevented the work from going ahead and Scott never lived to

W. A. Scott's drawing for the Basilica

see even the beginning of the grand building he had conceived.
After his death in 1921 the plans were entrusted to the architect T.
J. Cullen. Under Cullen's direction the work finally began in 1925.

By the time that Scott received the Lough Derg commission
he had already developed an individual style which came to be
known as Hiberno-Romanesque. The main features of this style
– rounded arches, round-tower motifs and multi-arched door-
ways – owe a great deal to Irish church architecture of the Middle
Ages. Scott combined these elements with his own individual
ideas. In his design for the Lough Derg church he incorporated
medieval elements into an unusual and striking octagonal plan
surmounted by a pointed octagonal dome which to this day
dominates the island skyline. From the outside, the building
projects a sense of massiveness and a rugged strength which is
enhanced by the rough stone of the exterior walls. Inside, the
impression is of a great enclosed space, which might well be
imagined as a great man-made cave.

The Basilica

In keeping with the austerity of the pilgrimage itself, the interior is very plain. This starkness was further emphasised when the sanctuary of the church was redesigned in 1988. Where previously the furniture and fittings had been conceived in a somewhat ornate neo-Celtic design, with very unsatisfactory additions to meet the requirements of the reformed liturgy, the new arrangement provided not only greater space for the celebration of the liturgy but also created a simplicity in keeping with the rest of the interior. The sanctuary furniture was specially commissioned in plain white marble. The tabernacle is a modern design based on the shape of the shrine of Saint Patrick's Bell, now in the National Museum of Ireland. It is balanced in the overall scheme by a lectern which is used both by the cantor who leads the singing during the daytime celebrations and the pilgrims who lead the Station Prayers during the night.

The original Sanctuary

A focal point in the whole arrangement is a massive cross, erected at the rear of the sanctuary. Designed by Imogen Stuart, the cross is simple yet very striking. It is carved from wood and is based on the design of the penal crosses used by Irish Catholics during the eighteenth and early nineteenth centuries. It is worth mentioning two interesting features of the cross. Below the figure of Christ the artist incorporates the symbols of the cock and the pot. These images recall an old Christian legend that was retold in various forms. One version has it that on the day of the resurrection the wife of Judas was preparing a meal. On being told that the Lord had risen from the dead, she refused to believe it. At that, the bird that she was cooking flew out of the pot crying, *'Mac na hÓighe slán!'*, 'The Son of the Virgin is alive!' In this way the design of the cross inspires reflection both on the passion of Christ and its glorious consequence.

This coupling of suffering and glory is also suggested by the way in which the artist has portrayed the halo around the head of Jesus. Here she has carved right through the wood, creating a

The Sanctuary redesigned in 1988

space through which light can shine. The intensity of Christ's pain and the darkness of his death cannot obliterate the hope of what is to follow.

The one concession to vivid and flamboyant colour in the Basilica is the series of stained glass windows which were created by the renowned Irish artist Harry Clarke. The windows contain representations of the fourteen Stations of the Cross. Each window is filled with a brilliantly coloured image of one of the apostles, with Our Lady and Saint Paul added to bring the number to fourteen. Each Station is depicted in the centre of each window on a delicately coloured insert which is held by the attendant saint. The impact of these windows, especially when the light of the setting sun pours through them, is quite magical in the contrast which they create with the overall restraint of the church's interior.

As with all building work on the island, the construction of the church was both technically and physically demanding, not least because limitations of space on the island demanded that the main body of the building had to be constructed on one hundred and twenty-three pillars of reinforced concrete sunk into the bed of the lake. The building work took four years to complete and cost £80,000. Although the church was in use for the pilgrimage season of 1930, the ceremony of consecration did not take place until 12 May 1931. On the following Sunday a special Mass of Thanksgiving was celebrated in the presence of Cardinal MacRory, the Papal Nuncio and many clerical and lay dignitaries. The distinguished guests were afterwards entertained at a banquet in the island boathouse. The church itself had been honoured with the title of a Minor Basilica by Pope Pius XI, for which reason the same Pope's coat of arms is fixed over the central entrance to the church.

Although the present day Basilica may seem remote from the original primitive cave, there is a clear continuity between the two. The vigil on Lough Derg has always been associated with a particular building. Just as the old accounts of the pilgrimage describe how at the beginning of his time of vigil the pilgrim was led to the cave by the prior and shut in for the night, so also do present-day pilgrims make their way to the Basilica at the start of their vigil. Once the pilgrims have been seated, the prior and staff depart and the great doors of the church are closed, the pilgrims abandoned to their night of prayer in the modern version of the ancient cave. In the Basilica the pilgrims of today face much the same struggle as their predecessors in medieval times. Although it is a long time since any visions were reported, it is worth noting that not all the pilgrims of the Middle Ages were accorded the dubious privilege of such experiences. We have already referred to the frustration endured by the monk of Eymstadt, but the modern pilgrim is more likely to identify with the experience of a certain Sir William Lisle, who journeyed to Lough Derg towards the end of the fourteenth century. Sir William described how he and his companion were admitted to the cave and began their vigil:

> They entered into the hole and were closed in at the sun going down and abode there all night, and the next morning issued out again at the sun-rising. Then he said how that when he and his fellow were entered and past the gate that was called the Purgatory of Saint Patrick, and that they were

descended and gone down three or four paces, descending down as into a cellar, a certain hot vapour rose against them and strake so into their heads, that they were fain to sit down on the stairs, which are of stone. And after they had sat there a season, they had great desire to sleep, and so fell asleep and slept there all night.'

Having presumably been through what was then a fifteen day fast coupled with a daunting regime of prayer, it is hardly surprising that Sir William and his friend should have succumbed to fatigue. The same factors may also provide a reasonable explanation for at least some of the visionary experiences of the time. But all pilgrims, then as now, have to contend with the twin demons of exhaustion and discouragement. The vigil, if no longer the occasion of visions or terrors, remains a trial for the strongest of bodies and the stoutest of hearts.

*Arriving at the Ferry House, early in the twentieth century.
The new women's hostel can be seen on the island, and, of course,
there was no basilica yet.*

CHAPTER THREE

The Journey to the Island

The pilgrimage season on Lough Derg is limited to the period between 1 June and the 15 August each year. After the closing of the cave in 1497 it seems that a longer season, beginning on 1 May, was the norm. This was reduced in the early nineteenth century to the present limits. At one point, between 1869 and 1880, the season was shortened further, lasting only from 1 July to 15 August, but the pressure of pilgrim numbers led to the previous arrangement being reintroduced. Since 1992 the island has been opened for one-day retreats outside the pilgrimage season. These days in May, the second half of August and the month of September, do not involve fasting or the Station Prayers. Taking advantage of the renewed facilities on the island, they provide an opportunity for a day of prayer on Lough Derg, especially for those who are unable to undertake the pilgrimage proper. The brevity of the pilgrimage season is easily explained by the harshness and unpredictability of the weather conditions outside of the summer months. Even in summer pilgrims may find that stormy winds, driving rain and unseasonal temperatures add to the burdens already imposed by the penances.

The length of the pilgrimage has varied throughout its history. The story of the Knight Owein tells that the custom was to spend fifteen days in prayer and fasting before the vigil in the cave, followed by another fifteen days afterwards. The earliest records tend to agree on fifteen days as the normal duration of the pilgrimage. By the later Middle Ages, however, the length of the pilgrimage seems to have become fixed at nine days. This was certainly the case when the Papal Nuncio Francesco Chiericati visited the island in 1517. The nine days of fasting were followed by the twenty-four hour vigil in the cave. This remained the pattern until the early nineteenth century. At this time, as the penal laws disappeared, there gradually came about a reduction in the duration of the pilgrimage. The reason for this is unclear, although it may have been the result of the increase in the numbers of people making the pilgrimage. At first the reduction seems to have been optional, or at least dependent on the severity of the penance imposed by the pilgrim's confessor. The Catholic Bishop of Clogher, James Murphy, writing in 1804, stated that pilgrims made 'a three, six, or nine days' station according to the nature of their vow or obligation, and in case of no vow or obligation, 'according to their devotion'. Certainly by the middle of the nineteenth century the normal length of the pilgrimage was three days, as it remains to this day.

Fasting

During the three days of pilgrimage the pilgrim observes a strict fast which begins at midnight on the night before arriving at the island. The Lough Derg fast has its roots in the long tradition of fasting in the Christian church. Even before the time of Christ, fasting was commonplace among the Jews. In the Old Testament fasting is most frequently associated with sorrow for sin and turning to God in times of distress. It was often accompanied by wailing, lamentation, walking barefoot and wearing sackcloth and ashes. In the Jewish Law, however, fasting was only laid down as obligatory on one day of the year, the Day of Atonement, when the people of Israel pray for purification and forgiveness from sin. The first Christians carried over many religious observances from their Jewish background and fasting was one of the most important of these. Following the Jewish tradition of fasting twice a week, the early Christians fasted on Wednesdays and Fridays of every week as well as in preparation for the major feasts of the year such as Easter and Christmas. Fasting was also prescribed as a public penance for serious sins.

Precise customs and regulations about fasting varied in the different parts of the Christian world but nowhere were they more rigorous than in the early monastic communities. In the eastern monasteries of Egypt, many of the monks and hermits subsisted only on a diet of bread, salt and water, as well as observing frequent days of complete abstinence from all food. The harshness of these practices was matched, and in many cases exceeded, in the Celtic monasteries. In his account of St Patrick's Purgatory, H of Saltrey retells a story which echoes the eastern tradition and also testifies to the existence of a long tradition of fasting associated with the monastery at Lough Derg. He recounts the tale of a prior of the monastery who lived some time after the death of St Patrick. This prior was so old that he had only one tooth left in his head. He was a very pious and saintly man, who longed for death to release him into God's glory. The account concludes:

> … the canons often heard angels in the old man's cell singing around him. And their song had these words: 'Blessed are you and blessed is the tooth that is in your mouth, which has never been touched by delectable food.' For his food was dry bread and salt and his drink was cold water. However he departed happily to the Lord, as he had wished.

Other early accounts of Lough Derg support the impression that, whatever about the pilgrims, the monks of those times knew the meaning of penance. Peter of Cornwall, writing in 1200, states that:

> There is in that small island a small chapel, where old men dwell permanently living a monastic life, who drink nothing but water mixed with milk and in the Lenten season they always feed on oaten bread containing a third part of ashes.

Traditionally, pilgrims to Lough Derg have been allowed one meal only on each day of their pilgrimage. When the nine-day pilgrimage was the norm, pilgrims were forbidden to take any food at all on the day before the twenty-four hour vigil, during the vigil itself, or on the following day. The modern pilgrimage regulations are less severe, allowing one meal on each of the three days, although on the first day of the pilgrimage the meal may not be taken until at least one Station Prayer has been completed.

The Refectory

To some people the description of what is provided on
Lough Derg as a 'meal' might appear to be stretching the meaning of the word more than a little. The menu consists of dry
toasted bread, plain oatcakes and black tea or coffee. The inclus-
ion of oatcakes is a continuing link to the original diet of the
monks as recorded by Peter of Cornwall. Until the end of the
nineteenth century only coarse oatmeal bread and water were
permitted. The water was taken from the lake, boiled in a large
cauldron and served hot. On account of the presence of impuri-
ties in the water it emerged a reddish colour and was commonly
referred to as 'Lough Derg wine'. The practice of drinking hot

The old boiler for 'Lough Derg Soup'

water throughout the pilgrimage persists to this day. Before the recent renovations on the island, a large copper boiler sat over an open turf fire in the men's hostel. Water drawn from this was frequently flavoured with salt and pepper, producing what was familiarly known as 'Lough Derg soup'. The introduction of black tea, and more recently black coffee, marks something of a softening of the fasting regulations. Moreover, the pilgrim is allowed at each meal to eat as much as he or she wants, or can stomach. On a slightly different note, some first-time pilgrims express surprise that smoking is permitted on the island. This has, however, always been the case, and at least in the present day this is confined to certain areas. As far back as 1701, it is recorded that the pilgrims smoked tobacco even in the confined space of the cave during the vigil, a practice which to some modern sensibilities would be considered almost a capital crime.

The boat to the island

Already fasting from midnight, the pilgrim arrives at the shore of the lake. In former times many pilgrims travelled to Lough Derg on foot, sometimes for many miles. Some made a point of going barefoot out of devotion; others out of necessity. Their journey often took them over very inhospitable terrain, but this was considered as very much a part of the complete pilgrimage experience. As the pilgrims approached the lake they removed their hats and shoes and waited for the boatmen to ferry them over to the island.

Originally the boats were owned and run by private individuals as profit-making concerns. The lack of proper regulation and supervision, as well as the keen competition between the various boatmen, meant that the crossing always involved a certain degree of risk. It is surprising that so few accidents occurred. The most notable disaster was the infamous boating tragedy of 12 July 1795.

It was a Sunday morning. Many people had gathered at the shore of the lake, waiting to be taken across to the island. Some were prospective pilgrims, others simply wishing to attend Mass on the island. At about eleven o'clock the ferryman, named Johnston, loaded up one of the boats. There were ninety-three passengers on board. The main boatman's name was MacTeague, and it is said that he disregarded concerns expressed by some of the passengers about the condition of his boat. It is said that just before the boat was to leave a man arrived at the quay in a hurry. He called to his son, who was on the boat, to leave at once and come home. The young man protested, but his father insisted, saying that he had had a warning in a dream the night before that his son's life was in danger. The son reluctantly left with his father. The still-crowded boat set out across the lake without much incident until it began to pass Friar's Island, a very short distance from the quay at Station Island. At this point some of the passengers noticed that the boat was taking on water. They shouted out to the boatmen, who ignored them, thinking that they were so close to the quay that they would reach it easily. But now the other passengers began to notice that the level of water inside the boat was rising rapidly. Fear and confusion led to panic. People began to stand up in the boat with the result that the boat capsized. It quickly sank. The depth of the water at this point was about ten feet. Hardly any of the people in the boat could swim and in any case were so overcome by their panic that they grappled with each other in the water. Only three pilgrims survived. The rest, including the boatmen, drowned. Meanwhile on the island quay a crowd of people watched in horror as the tragedy unfolded only metres away. Their shock was so great that no-one thought of taking the boats at the quay and attempting to rescue anyone.

Later the bodies were recovered from the lake. About twenty were buried in a mass grave on Friar's Island. Others, mainly local people, were buried together in nearby Templecarne graveyard. The remaining bodies were claimed by relatives. Some of these were very poor and came from the far west of Ireland. Many accounts paint an unforgettably poignant picture of these poor people travelling home over the mountains carry-

The small wooden cross found in the hand of Miss O'Donnell who drowned in the 1795 tragedy

ing the dead bodies on their backs. The incident lived long in the memories of the local people and gave rise to several superstitions, the most persistent of which is that it is bad luck to share a boat to the island with a red-haired woman. A more tangible relic of the tragedy is preserved in St Mary's church on the island. Here in a glass case can be seen a small, roughly-carved wooden cross, dated 1792. It was found clutched in the hand of one of the corpses, identified as a Miss O'Donnell from Derry.

Although the 1795 tragedy was the last instance of loss of life, the organisation of boats to the island continued to create problems throughout the nineteenth century. There are records of boatmen making money conducting tours to the island during the pilgrimage season in spite of the objections of the prior. In 1829 the pilgrimage was closed down for the season because in previous seasons the boatmen had established the practice of having dancing and drunken revels on the lake shore. It was not until 1917 that the church authorities bought out the ferry rights from the local landlord and finally gained complete control over the boats and the boatmen.

CHAPTER FOUR

The Station Prayers

When the fasting pilgrims arrive on the island, their first duty is to go to the hostel buildings, claim a cubicle and remove their shoes and socks. Their feet will remain bare until just before their departure on the morning of the third day of pilgrimage. They immediately make their way to St Patrick's Basilica to begin the first of the Station Prayers. The word Station usually refers to the combination of prayers and movements which make up the Station Prayer, but is also often used as a term for the pilgrimage as a whole. The precise origin of the Station Prayer is unclear. Certainly early sources, such as the *Tractatus* of H of Saltrey, make clear that long periods of prescribed prayer were an indispensable element of the pilgrimage. In these early accounts prayers are described as an essential preparation for the night of trial in the vigil cave and an act of thanksgiving for safe deliverance from the cave itself. We are not told if the prayers followed a fixed pattern at that time, but such a pattern did develop over the centuries and has persisted, with some modifications, to the present day.

In the accounts of the later Middle Ages we begin to see a much greater emphasis being placed on the types of penitential exercises which were laid down for the pilgrims. This is related to the fact that the experience of visions in the purgatory cave was on the wane. In these later accounts there are references to practices which will be familiar to pilgrims today. The Papal Nuncio Chiericati, writing in 1517, mentions the fast and also the practices of praying while doing rounds of cells associated with St Patrick, St Brigid and St Columba.

That there was a prescribed set of prayers and exercises is apparent from the accounts of Chiericati and others. It is reported that, after the suppression of the pilgrimage on the island by Spottiswoode in 1632, pilgrims continued to come to the shore of the lake and performed the whole sequence of prayers and exercises there, until access to the island was regained. This assumes an established and well-known structure of prayer and this is confirmed in the written accounts of the period.

The prayers laid down for the pilgrims had to be said three times a day for (at that time) nine days, after which the pilgrims undertook the vigil. Bishop Hugh MacMahon reported in 1714 that the pilgrims

> spend nine days living on one meal each day of oaten bread and water. They rest upon the cold ground, walk barefoot, and their feet are frequently cut and bleeding. Thrice each

At St Patrick's Cross

day do they visit the different stations over a rough path strewn with sharp pebbles, a considerable part of which is covered with water knee-deep.

Each of the Station Prayers also followed a set pattern. This pattern is clearly laid out in one of the earliest printed guides for pilgrims, that of the Dominican priest Dominic Brullaghan, produced in 1726. Brullaghan describes the Station Prayer in three parts: 'Of the Stations about the Chapel', 'Of the Stations about the seven *(sic)* penitential beds', and 'Of the Stations in the water'. The Station today follows precisely the same sequence.

The pilgrim begins the Station with a visit to the Basilica, the successor of previous churches on the island. Here he spends a moment in prayer before the Blessed Sacrament, before leaving the Basilica and going to kneel at St Patrick's Cross just outside. The cross itself is of little interest, being simply a plain metal cross. It is the stone shaft into which it is set that is historically noteworthy. It dates back to the early Middle Ages and is a relic of the monastic settlement on the lake. The original stone cross has been lost, probably in the attack of 1632. The existing shaft is decorated with spiral carving and an octagonal capital. At the cross, the pilgrim recites one Our Father, one Hail Mary and one Creed. These three prayers are the constituent elements of the Station and will have been repeated many times before its end. It is traditional for the pilgrim to kiss the cross before the next part of the Station.

The pilgrim then goes to the side of the Basilica, into which is set a large stone with a simple carved cross. This is known as St Brigid's Cross. Its age is uncertain, but it is probably medieval. Along with the other old stone memorials inlaid to the wall of the Basilica, this cross had previously been set into the wall of the old St Patrick's church and forms part of the few historical relics which survived the more turbulent years of Lough Derg's history. Kneeling before St Brigid's Cross, the pilgrim recites three Our Fathers, three Hail Marys and a Creed. This combination of prayers is used repeatedly throughout the Station and this has been the case since at least the sixteenth century. The pilgrim then performs one of the more striking Lough Derg rituals. Standing with her back to the cross, she stretches out her arms in the sign of the cross and says three times: 'I renounce the World, the Flesh and the Devil.' This ritual is a reminder of the Christian baptismal promises and also recalls the ancient ascetic practice of standing, sometimes for hours, facing the east in the attitude of Christ on the cross. Brullaghan talks of kissing the cross as a sign of taking up the cross to follow Christ and continues:

> Likewise after we kiss the same cross, before we depart from it, we touch it with our shoulders; by which we signify, that we ought to persevere in carrying our cross to the end.

Leaving St Brigid's Cross, the pilgrim embarks upon four circuits of the Basilica, praying seven decades of the Rosary and one Creed. Originally the pilgrim was supposed to walk around the church seven times, but this was reduced to four when the present much larger church was built. Brullaghan, in typically allegorical fashion, interprets the spiritual symbolism of this part of the Station in several ways. The pilgrim is here atoning

At St Brigid's Cross

for the seven deadly sins which we all commit on the seven days of the week. He is also remembering the sacrifice of Christ, who shed his blood for us seven times: at his circumcision, in the garden of Gethsemane, when he was scourged, when he was crowned with thorns, when his garments were stripped from his body, when he was nailed to the cross and, finally, when his side was pierced with a spear.

Having completed the prayers around the church, the pilgrim moves on to the penitential beds which are located at the centre of the island. Of all the aspects of the Lough Derg pilgrimage, the one which appears most strange to the outside observer or the first-time pilgrim is the sight of the bare-footed pilgrims doggedly wending their way around the rocky circles of the penitential beds while mouthing a seemingly endless litany of prayers. These penitential beds are the remnants of the cells to which Chiericati referred. They are the oldest remaining structures on the island and represent a tangible link to its Celtic past, both in the structures themselves and the acts of penance and prayer which take place on them. It is thought that they are the remains of old beehive cells used by the monastic community of

Lough Derg as far back as the ninth century. They are mentioned as early as 1186 by Gerald of Wales and many of the accounts since then testify to their importance as the focus of the pilgrimage penances. They appear on Thomas Carve's map of 1666 much as they are today, with the same saints' names attached to them.

Each bed consists of a low circular wall with a small gap as an entrance. The interior of the bed is simply a floor of rough bare rocks, in some cases the bedrock of the island itself. The rocks are very uneven, inflicting suitable punishment on the pilgrims' bare feet, not to mention the risk of slipping on them in wet weather. The Protestant minister John Richardson, in an otherwise harshly critical account of the pilgrimage written in 1727, was still impressed that people could endure the penances on these beds. He remarks that:

the Irish believe that the saints lay several nights upon these beds by way of penance for their own sins and the sins of the people, which, if true, the hardness of their lodging made the penance very severe.

He adds that the beds are:

so rugged and thick set with small pointed stones that the greatest saint in the church of Rome could not bear it now and much less take any rest upon them.

The crude appearance of the penitential beds even moved an American visitor in 1857 to offer a substantial sum of money to the diocese in order to have the beds completely renovated in cut stone. The offer was politely declined.

At the centre of each bed stands a bronze cross bearing the figure of Christ and the name of the saint to whom the bed is dedicated. These crosses were installed in the 1870s. The six beds are named after Saints Brigid, Brendan, Catherine, Columba, Patrick and, in the case of the last bed, a double dedication to the great abbot saints of the area, Saint Davog of Lough Derg and Saint Molaise of Devenish. The only non-Irish saint represented is Saint Catherine. This is probably Saint Catherine of Alexandria to whom there was widespread devotion in

The penitential beds

Ireland in the Middle Ages. She was originally a martyr in the fourth century who, according to legend, was killed by being broken on a wheel, thus giving her name to a popular firework as well as this rocky circle on Lough Derg.

The pilgrim begins at Saint Brigid's bed, the one furthest from the Basilica. Here he recites three Our Fathers, three Hail Marys and the Creed, while walking around the outside of the bed. These prayers are then repeated three times – once while kneeling at the entrance to the bed, once walking around the inside of the bed and finally while kneeling at the cross in the centre of the bed. The pilgrim then moves on to the next bed and performs the same exercises. The last two beds, those of Saint Patrick and Saints Davog and Molaise, are conjoined and therefore the outer circuit of the two beds requires the recitation of six Our Fathers, six Hail Marys and the Creed.

The next part of the station prayer takes place at the Water's Edge, the shore of the lake beside the penitential beds. Here the pilgrim is required to stand and say five Our Fathers, five Hail Marys and the Creed. He then kneels and repeats the same prayers. This ritual beside the lake is a relic of earlier practices which in some cases involved the pilgrim becoming completely submerged in the water. In the late Middle Ages, it appears to have been the practice for the pilgrims to immerse themselves naked three times in the lake on emerging from the cave at the end of the vigil. Papal Nuncio Chiericati in 1517 reported that pilgrims sometimes remained up to their necks in the water for several hours. By 1714, when Bishop Hugh MacMahon wrote his account, it seems that pilgrims were only required to dip their heads in the water three times. The traditional procedure on completion of the penitential beds was to wade into the lake to a series of sharp stones; to first stand, then kneel on the stones and say the required prayers. The pilgrim then moved on to a larger, smoother stone further out in the lake. This stone was known as the 'monk's stone of penance' and was supposed to bear the imprint of the knees of Patrick himself. It was believed to have healing properties, bringing relief to the sore knees and feet of the pilgrim. Brullaghan, in his description of the 'Stations in the Water' writes:

> Having finished the stations of the penal beds, we begin the station of the water … we go round the stones, standing in the water three times, to satisfy for the sins of our will, memory and understanding; saying, in the meantime, five Paters, five Aves and one Creed, to redeem the punishment due to the sins of our five outward senses; then humbly kneeling on the sharp stones … from whence we advance to a round stone, a distance out in the lough, on which we stand, and say one Pater, one Ave and one Creed to signify that we beg one thing of God, to wit, life everlasting.

In the later edition of 1820 a footnote comments: 'No person is now permitted to go into the water.' It appears that the practice of pilgrims bathing in the lake had alarmed the increasingly delicate sensibilities of the clerical authorities and had been forbidden as a potential source of scandal.

At the water's edge

The conclusion of the Station involves a return to Saint Patrick's Cross to repeat the prayers said there earlier. The pilgrim then finishes the Station in the Basilica with five Our Fathers, five Hail Marys and a Creed, traditionally offered for the intentions of the Pope. It is only after one full Station has been completed that the pilgrim is permitted to take the meal of the first day of pilgrimage. In keeping with a long-standing tradition, the pilgrimage contains nine Stations in all. Three are made on the first day after arriving on the island, four during the night of the Vigil, one during the rest of the second day and the final Station on the morning of the third day just before leaving the island. During the night of the Vigil, the Stations are performed inside the Basilica, following precisely the order of the daytime Stations and reproducing all the necessary postures, gestures and movement. The fact that it is possible to complete the Station prayers away from the penitential beds is one reason why pilgrims in the seventeenth century were able to continue making a pilgrimage of sorts at the lake shore after the destruction of 1632. In a similar way, the pilgrimage was undertaken in unusual circumstances on two occasions in more recent times.

During the political upheavals of the 1920s a large group of prisoners was interned in a camp at Ballykinlar in County Down. Some of the prisoners had previously made the pilgrimage to Lough Derg and decided to ask permission of the governor to carry out the exercises of the pilgrimage in the camp. A large number of other prisoners also asked to be included. The chaplain to the camp requested and received approval for the idea from the Prior of Lough Derg. The governor agreed to allow the 'pilgrimage' to go ahead, although without the twenty-four hour vigil. The whole exercise lasted from 11 to 15 August 1921. The men kept the fast according to the pilgrimage regulations and added on three extra Stations to compensate for the lack of a vigil. A report was sent to the Prior who had special commemorative medals struck and presented to each of the men who had taken part.

A similar episode took place two years later. This involved one hundred and ninety-four internees on board the prison ship *Argenta,* moored in Belfast Lough in August 1923. Once again the men followed faithfully the order and regulations of the pilgrimage. The prison chaplain sent details of the incident, including a list of the men's names, to the Prior who once again had a medal produced to mark the occasion.

The completion of the final Station on Lough Derg is a moment of great relief. At this point the pilgrims are permitted to put

307

"On board the Argenta"

John Donnigan	Ballybannon	Down	Patrick McGuirk	Egling
John Greenan	Banbridge		James Kelly	Drapers
John McAllinden	Laurencetown	"	Thomas Lartkin	Belleag
John Doran	Loughisland	"	John Grant	Killat
John Bell	Crossgar	"	Michael O'Kane	Limer
Edward McGlennon	Loughisland	"	James Horner	Derry
Patrick McGinn	Killkeel	"	Wm McCloskey	Dung
Stephen O'Hagan	Killkeel	"	Thomas Corrigan	Enniski
Edward O'Connolly	Laurancetown	"	Joseph Dolan	Belcoo
Frank Harper	Killkeel (Greencastle)	"	John Cassidy (Carrigan)	Ennis
William Byrne	Downpatrick	"	John Nethercott	Ennisk
Henry Wolfe	Downpatrick	"	John Quinn	Clones
Sam Cunningham	Downpatrick	"	John Murphy Cadilla	Roslea
Wan Wallace	Downpatrick	"	Wm McLoughlin Derghag	E. Ennis
Patrick Hughes	Rostrevor	"	Edward Gray Pettencier	Lemp
Peter Murphy	Corkhill Co Armagh	"	Patrick Murphy Derghae	E. Ennis
John Quinn	Lurgan (Derghae)	"	Thomas Cox	Ennis
Brian Naughey	Lurgan		Hugh Gilroy Army	Drumt
John Cosgrove	Lisley Armagh	"	Henry McCaulay Yrmea	E. Ennis
James Connolly	Armagh (City)	"	Edward Brady Aughn	E. Enne
Terence Toner	Nton Hamilton	"	John Meehan Pagel Sy	E. Enn
Jas Kairns	Lurgan (Ballymany)	"	Patrick Leonard Derghae	Ennis
John O'Hagan	Armagh city	"	Felix Hackett	Ennis
Henry McKenna	Casagh	"	Edward Fitzpatrick Newry	Rathm
Edward Brennan	Derrynoose	"		
Hugh McKenna	Lurgan	"		
Brian McArdle	Mullybawn	"	Complete total	194
Joseph Conlon	Markethill			
John Morgan	Markethill	"	The four names marked thus —
James McKeown	Lurgan (Derghagh)		obliged to abandon the pilgr.
Denis Lavelle N?	Newry Mullaghlawn	"	owing to weakness.
Patrick Donnolly	Derryhaus	"	
Charles Bryson	Limavady Co Derry	"	The total number of prisoners .

An extract from the ledger on the Argenta Pilgrimage

on their shoes and prepare to leave the island. As the boat pulls away from the quay the pilgrims sing the hymn to Saint Patrick, *Hail Glorious Saint Patrick*. It is only in recent times that this hymn has supplanted the traditional *Farewell Hymn to Lough Derg*. This nineteenth-century composition fell out of general use in the latter part of the twentieth century although it was still sung on the last day of the pilgrimage season at least until the 1970s. Perhaps the sentiments expressed did not quite reflect the feelings of most departing pilgrims:

So fare thee well Lough Derg;
Shall I ever see thee more?
My heart is filled with sorrow
To leave thy sainted shore.
Until life's days have passed away,
With pleasure shall I dwell
On the happy days I spent with thee,
Lough Derg, fare thee well!

CHAPTER FIVE

The Spirit of the Pilgrimage

> In an age of scepticism and unbelief, it is refreshing to turn aside from the busy paths of the world, in order to contemplate the sanctuaries of religion and the holy shrines of pilgrimage, round which are encircled the most sacred associations and the most venerable traditions.

It is interesting at the beginning of the twenty-first century to reflect on the perspective of one hundred years ago, when Father D. O'Connor wrote these opening words to his book on Lough Derg. It may seem to us at the dawn of the third millennium that scepticism and unbelief are far more characteristic of our own time than the late nineteenth century. On the other hand it is useful to note how, throughout the compass of human history, spiritual questing and questioning remain a constant feature of human experience. For all human beings the struggle to make sense of existence is the driving force of what is in effect the interior pilgrimage of the spirit. Sometimes this experience can be put into words but more often it is best expressed in action, through the physical expression of ambition, emotion, altruism or faith. The great religious pilgrimages have in common the fact that they are all physical expressions of human religious faith. Not many have given witness to such expression for as long and as physically as the pilgrimage to Lough Derg.

The most remarkable thing about Lough Derg has been its ability to survive the worst vicissitudes of its history and to continue to draw the questing pilgrim all the way to the remote north-west of Ireland. Why is it that the spirit of Lough Derg has remained alive and vibrant into the third Christian millennium? The answer lies in the nature of that unique spirit and its ability to preserve tradition while embracing change. The thread which

links the modern pilgrimage with its origins remains unbroken, but it is woven through a fabric that is fascinatingly diverse in colour and texture, as we have already seen.

Even from its origins, this pilgrimage has stood somewhat apart from the other great pilgrimages of the Christian world. Lough Derg was not a place which in itself held great significance for the fervent Christian. It did not have the glamour of direct association with Christ himself that the sites of the Holy Land did. Nor was it hallowed by the bones of a great saint such as drew hordes of medieval pilgrims to the shrines of Peter and Paul at Rome or James at Compostella. The somewhat tenuous link with Patrick, a relatively minor national apostle, would hardly have been much of an attraction. Lough Derg possessed none of the great and holy relics which proliferated in the Middle Ages and were considered essential centre-pieces for any successful pilgrimage shrine. It did not offer the promise of healing or the guarantee of salvation. In its earliest days it seems to have simply provided the monks and other pious Christians with the opportunity to retreat from the secular world and atone for sin through penance, fasting and prayer. For some this may have been seen as a final preparation for the next life and this may indeed have prepared the way for the perception of Lough Derg in the medieval tradition as not just a place of preparation for the next world but a point of contact with it. We have seen that the pilgrimage reached a peak of medieval fame on account of the often lurid stories of the visions which were to be seen there and these certainly sustained the popularity of the pilgrimage for several hundred years. And yet there was certainly a pilgrimage in existence before the Knight Owein made his momentous visit, and this same pilgrimage did not disappear when the visions ceased and the reports of them faded in Christian memory. The fact is that the pilgrimage to Lough Derg has in many ways been coloured and perceived by the spirit of the age but has never been hostage to it. It is rather the case that, in the different phases of its history, Lough Derg has addressed the pilgrim mind in a way that has been both profound and accessible.

The visionary period of the pilgrimage, from the time of the Knight Owein in the twelfth century to the aftermath of the Suppression of Alexander VI in 1497, can be best understood in terms of the developments in Christian thought and above all the view of the world which prevailed at that time.

In the medieval European mind, the known world did not extend much beyond the confines of Europe itself. The continents of Asia to the east and Africa to the south were vast and dark unknowns, while the Atlantic Ocean to the west was simply the last expanse of water which lay between humanity and the edge of the world. The westernmost lands of the European continent therefore formed the true ends of the earth itself. Lough Derg, situated almost at the edge of the island of Ireland, was at the margins of the earth. In some of the medieval accounts of the pilgrimage we find this idea clearly expressed. Two letters accompanying the account of the pilgrimage of the Hungarian nobleman George Grissaphan in 1353 illustrate this well. In one, Prior Paul of Lough Derg dates his letter 7 December 1353 'in the monastery of the Purgatory of Saint Patrick, our patron, in the ends or final parts of the world'. In another, the then bishop of the diocese, Nicholas MacCathasaigh, identifies himself as the 'Bishop of Clogher, by the ends of the world'. It is not surprising that visions of the next world should come to be associated with a place at the margins of this one. Lough Derg could be perceived as lying at the threshold of the beyond, and the famous cave provided the gateway through which the pilgrim could gain access to the realms of the afterlife.

The visionary aspect of the pilgrimage can also be understood in the context of the religious preoccupations of the time. The often precarious nature of human existence in the Middle Ages, when threats of war, plague and famine were never far off, inevitably focused people's minds on the afterlife. The hope of an eternal blissful existence, in sharp contrast to the brief and brutish experience of earthly life, vied with fear of the agonising punishments which were the inevitable consequence of the sins of mankind. These preoccupations are reflected in the literature and art of the period, from the *Divine Comedy* of Dante to the paintings of Hieronymus Bosch. They are evident in the Todi fresco and help to explain the fascination of the visions in the cave at Lough Derg.

The end of the visionary period marks a shift in emphasis in the practice of the pilgrimage. The last detailed account of an experience of visions in the cave is that of another Hungarian pilgrim, Laurence Rathold, who made the pilgrimage in 1411. By the time of the visit of the Papal Nuncio Chiericati in 1517, the visionary aspect of the pilgrimage had all but disappeared. Chiericati mentions that two of his companions had such experiences in the cave, but he seems unconcerned with the details. Instead his account presents a picture of the pilgrimage which is far more focused on its penitential aspects. From this time on, the association of Lough Derg with visions of the next world virtually ceases. The cave becomes, or simply reverts to being the site of one element of the programme of penances on the island.

What brought about this change? It seems that a combination of circumstances was responsible. The suppression of the pilgrimage by Alexander VI in 1497, although short-lived, may have been a contributory factor. However, it is another contemporary event which may have been more influential. In 1492 Columbus had revealed the Americas to the peoples of Europe. As this age of discovery continued, the horizons of the world expanded. Lough Derg, which had appeared to be located at the very edge of the world, was now perceived as a small part of a much wider domain, where wonders of a more natural and tangible kind were to be found. At the same time, social and economic changes were also making an impact on the religious attitudes of the time. Already in the fifteenth century, new religious movements had encouraged the development of a more personal spirituality. These movements emphasised the idea that God was to be found as much through an interior journey of the soul as in the revelations of visions or the wondrous sights of the great pilgrimages.

This greater emphasis on an individual and highly personal spirituality, combined with the growing criticism of the extravagance and material corruption of the institutional church, led to a waning in the popularity of pilgrimages in general. The highly critical report on Lough Derg by the monk of Eymstadt in 1494 reflects these attitudes. The monk's chief complaint about the pilgrimage is the accusation of simony, that is the selling of spiritual things for monetary gain. This was one of the chief charges of corruption against the church generally at that time. According to the monk, at almost every stage of his pilgrimage money was demanded of him. He concluded that the whole pilgrimage was a fraud but that 'the inhabitants of the place were nonetheless asserting to visitors, for financial gain, that purgation of sins was still taking place there'. These changes in perception may well account not only for the disappearance of visionary literature concerning St Patrick's Purgatory, but also the decline in its international fame. We come across little evidence in the following centuries of any significant European interest in Lough Derg or many further accounts of importance by European pilgrims. From this point onwards, the pilgrimage was to be sustained mainly by the devotion of the Irish people.

The spirit of the age which led to the great religious upheaval of the Reformation made no small contribution to the resurgence of the original spirit of the pilgrimage as a penitential journey. It is possible to see the period of visions as an atypical phase in the development of the pilgrimage. The visions may have won an international reputation for Lough Derg, but they were never its reason for existing, nor were they the main reason why the majority of pilgrims had come there. As all the accounts make clear, the chief purpose of the pilgrimage was atonement for sin. If visions were granted, it was only to remind the pilgrim of the necessity for penance and the consequences for those who neglected it.

The essential spirit of Lough Derg as a place of penance for the forgiveness of sin is reflected in the name associated with it from the earliest times – Saint Patrick's Purgatory. By purgatory

was meant a place for the cleansing or purgation of sin. The association of the cave with the purgatory of the next world derived from the visionary accounts of the Knight Owein and those who followed him. These stories are important witnesses to the development of the doctrine of purgatory in the eleventh century and afterwards. They express in terms of popular imagery the growing notion of purgatory as a third place in the next world, intermediate between heaven and hell. More importantly for the subsequent development of the pilgrimage, this belief in purgatory as a place of purification of souls before their reception into heaven brought to the fore in the Catholic tradition the importance of prayer for the souls of the dead. The idea that the prayers, and even more so the penances, of the faithful on earth could relieve the sufferings or shorten the time of pain of the souls in purgatory had a profound impact on the spirit of the Lough Derg pilgrimage. This is why, even when visions of the next world ceased to be a feature of the pilgrimage, the next world itself still remained at the forefront of the pilgrimage spirit.

This focus is evident from the sixteenth century onwards in the emphasis which was increasingly placed on the indulgences which could be obtained by completing the pilgrimage exercises. The diligent pilgrim could obtain the remission of the pains of purgatory for one or more of the Holy Souls either partially (for a specified length of time) or in certain circumstances completely (by virtue of a plenary indulgence). An early witness to this is found in a letter written by the Prior of Lough Derg, Donatus McGrath, in 1507. Donatus refers to the 'indulgences of divers Roman pontiffs and other bishops granted to our place, which sum up to ten thousand, six hundred and seven years'. These indulgences could be obtained, not only by the pilgrims, but also by those who assisted them in their pilgrimage. In the succeeding centuries the granting and renewal of indulgences was seen as a sign of special favour from the Pope. To gain all the available indulgences on the island was perceived as a major goal of the pilgrimage well into the twentieth century. Father O'Connor, writing towards the end of the nineteenth century, gives succinct expression to this view. Commenting on the Papal Indult of Pius IX (1870) by which a plenary indulgence was granted indefinitely to all Lough Derg pilgrims, he writes:

> The pious pilgrim to Lough Derg must feel heartfelt satisfaction in reading the above Indult, which may be regarded as the charter and title deed of the pilgrimage.

The concept of indulgences remained an important focus of the pilgrimage throughout the post-visionary period. But if the

accomplishment of the penitential exercises could assist the souls of the dead, they were also perceived as very beneficial to the souls of the living. By atoning for his own sins through penance, the fervent pilgrim could also hope to gain some remission for himself from the pains of purgatory. Cardinal Logue, addressing the pilgrims on Lough Derg in 1913, wryly confessed his own failure to avail of this opportunity:

> I often intended to come here and do some little thing to make up for my unruly life – but when the time came there was always some new duty to be discharged that made me put it off; but I hope before I die to be able to carry it out still … I believe that any person that goes through the routine here on Lough Derg, the penitential exercises, the fasting and the prayers to which so many indulgences are granted – I believe if he died after leaving it, he would have very little to suffer in the next world.

Even to this day the traditional belief persists that the pilgrim who completes the Lough Derg pilgrimage three times will be saved from eternal damnation.

The tale of the Knight Owein and the other visionary accounts of Lough Derg may have had the most striking impact on European religious consciousness, but throughout its history the pilgrimage to Saint Patrick's Purgatory has been the subject of spiritual reflection in prose and poetry. When the time of visions had passed, and the pilgrimage continued as a more sombre challenge of physical penance, it still managed to exert a fascination over the spiritual imagination. The spirit of the pilgrimage found expression not only through the exertions of the many pilgrims who braved its challenges, but also in the writings of those who found in it a source of inspiration. The earliest examples are to be found in the works of native Irish poets, some of which were preserved orally for some time before eventually being written down. The imagery in these poems focuses on the various elements of the pilgrimage, especially the vigil in the cave, and on the island location of the penitential exercises. These are often seen as symbols of the spiritual journey of the pilgrim. The pilgrim in the cave is buried with Christ, contemplating his sins, so that he can emerge with the Risen Christ, freed from all sin. References to the waters of the lake evoke the washing rituals which took place at the end of the vigil and develop the theme of spiritual cleansing. The sixteenth-century poet Tadhg Dall Ó hUiginn uses the metaphor of healing in his meditation on the pilgrimage. He describes Saint Patrick as the physician who helps to heal the wounds of sin. The cave is a house of remedy for the ills of the soul. On leaving the cave the pilgrim discards his garment of sickness and is fully restored in the healing waters of the lake.

It is interesting to note how strong the symbolism of baptism is in this tradition. Some poems directly compare the lake with the River Jordan in which Jesus was baptised. A similar idea is expressed rather differently in the commentary of Dominic Brullaghan (1726). Here the author plays on the name of the lake. Just as the Israelites crossed the Red Sea to freedom from slavery, so the pilgrim crosses the 'Red Lake' (Loch Dearg) to be freed from sin. In the ancient tradition of the Christian church, the crossing of the Red Sea was seen as an image of the saving waters of baptism. The symbolism of baptism is still an important element in the modern pilgrimage.

The meditations of the Gaelic poets and the pious allegories of Brullaghan and others each reflect the spirit of their own times. The polemics of Richardson, Otway and others bear witness to the fascination which the pilgrimage could exert even over those who were not in the least well disposed towards it. That same fascination has persisted to the present day, whether expressed through the poetry of Kavanagh and Heaney or in the increasing number of reports about the pilgrimage in print and on film. Is this a fascination simply with a curious relic of the past, or is it because the spirit of the pilgrimage still possesses the power to inspire in the third millennium of the Christian era? The fact that thousands of pilgrims, from Ireland and around the world, continue to journey to Lough Derg each year to pray and to undertake what is still a severe programme of penance would seem to provide the answer.

The ferry house on the occasion of the visit of Cardinal Logue, 1913

CHAPTER SIX

An Ancient Pilgrimage in a New Millennium

In many ways Lough Derg is a contradictory place. It contradicts the accepted values of the world, by offering to people the opposite of what human beings are supposed to want. Comfort, nourishment and sleep are discarded in favour of hardship, hunger and exhaustion. The exercises of the pilgrimage, viewed from the perspective of the modern age, appear to be baffling or even perverse. But the fact remains that this pilgrimage exerts a strong attraction on a remarkably diverse group of people, young and old, from widely varied social and cultural backgrounds.

This attraction cannot be ascribed to the island itself – it is a bleak and inhospitable place. Nor are pilgrims drawn to Lough Derg to see ancient relics or monuments. These, such as ever existed, have long since disappeared and there has never been any hesitation in demolishing and renewing the fabric of the island. The only real relics are the penitential beds themselves and their role is certainly more functional than aesthetic. The simple fact is that, for the pilgrims, Lough Derg is as much an experience as a place. The common expression is to say that one has 'done' Lough Derg rather than simply been there.

If Lough Derg has the power to speak in this way to the modern age, it is because, as in every age, it addresses a real spiritual need in human beings. Perhaps the most contradictory aspect of the Lough Derg pilgrimage is the fact that for many pilgrims, the need which it fulfils is to find some measure of peace. How this can come about through a severely penitential pilgrimage may be difficult to understand, but there are some factors which certainly contribute.

The nature of Pilgrimage

The first of these has to do with the nature of all pilgrimages. Becoming a pilgrim means first of all focusing upon a sacred place and making the decision to journey there. In embarking on this journey the pilgrim steps outside of ordinary everyday life, displacing himself from his usual surroundings and routine. In so doing, the goal of his journey is not just a sacred place but a sacred space in time which is quite distinct from normal existence. Entering into this new environment, the pilgrim undergoes an experience, which in some way changes him. This is a ritual experience, which involves the use of words, gestures and symbols to express in a physical way the spiritual reality of the experience. It is also a communal experience, since the pilgrim is only one of many who undergo the same process. Finally, the pilgrimage involves a return, a homeward journey which ends with the pilgrim once more taking up the life he left behind, but now strengthened and inspired by the journey he has undertaken. The pilgrimage is therefore not the abandonment and rejection of worldly life, but a means of enriching it.

The Faith of the Pilgrim

A second factor, and one which has the utmost importance in our understanding of the pilgrimage to Lough Derg, is faith. It is true that non-Christians and even atheists have come to Lough Derg and undergone the pilgrimage. The majority have departed with a sense of having benefited from the experience. But the fact remains that the pilgrimage has always been first and foremost a pilgrimage of Christian faith. The prayers used and the sacraments celebrated are those of the Catholic Church. But the pilgrim also experiences many symbols that are deeply rooted in the Christian history of pilgrimage and highly expressive of the Christian faith. For this reason the pilgrimage has a particular ambience, rhythm and resonance which communicate to the believing Christian.

Faith is also important as the motivating force which propels the pilgrim on his journey. The pilgrimage is undertaken in a spirit of faith which transforms the pilgrim's perception of what

it is he is doing and imbues it with a meaning beyond the purely physical experience.

Conversion

A final point to consider is that a pilgrimage is always a journey of conversion. The physical journey involved is the outward expression of the pilgrim's need to turn towards God and away from sin. What this means in effect is that the spiritual journey of the pilgrim has as its goal the reconciliation of the pilgrim with God. In the case of Catholic pilgrimages, this process is centred on the celebration of the sacraments of eucharist and reconciliation.

In the Lough Derg pilgrimage, all of these factors come into play. The pilgrim to Lough Derg is very conscious of leaving behind the concerns and habits of everyday life in order to make a journey to a sacred place. Even before the actual journey is begun, the pilgrimage fast from the night before marks the beginning of the process. The sense of separation from normal life is emphasised by the short voyage in the boat to the island. A boundary has been crossed: the pilgrim has entered a new world.

Removing of shoes and socks and the feeling of the cold ground with bare feet is more than just a physical experience. It too is a gesture of abandonment. As the pilgrim emerges barefoot from the hostel and prepares to begin the first station prayer, there begins a process of bonding. People often remark how quickly and easily a group of pilgrims, arriving the same day on Lough Derg, begin to form a cohesive unit. Even before the real exertions of the pilgrimage have forged links through shared experience, there is a sense of unity. Social distinctions, differences in age or culture or outlook lose the significance which they have in the world that has been left behind – all are equal, all are pilgrims.

Prayer

Once the first station is underway, the rhythm of the pilgrimage begins to take hold. In the stations the sense of journey is heightened. It is a journey that is marked out in the cycles of prayers and the circuits of the Basilica and penitential beds. The prayers forge their own rhythm which is more important than the words themselves. The prayer of the Lough Derg pilgrims is not a prayer of the lips or the mind; it is a prayer of the whole body.

Lough Derg challenges us to revise our notions of what prayer is by presenting us with a way of praying which is rarely practised in the world today. It owes its character to the Celtic origins of the pilgrimage, which give it its ascetic nature. It is the physical nature of prayer on Lough Derg that so clearly defines the spirit of the place. The prayer of fasting, vigil and physical penance is the unbroken thread in the long history of the pilgrimage and an authentic expression of Celtic Christian spirituality. At the same time, the Station Prayer is characterised by symbolic movements and gestures which consciously or unconsciously raise the mind to God. The station is dominated by movement in circles. The circle of course is an image of eternity, having neither beginning nor end. At the penitential beds, larger circles become smaller ones as the pilgrim is physically drawn towards the centre. It is appropriate that at the centre of each bed the pilgrim is faced with the image of Christ on the cross. The Station

itself comes full circle as the pilgrim returns at the end to St Patrick's Cross where the Station began.

The image of the cross forms an important symbolic element in the Station Prayer. When the pilgrim stands with his back to St Brigid's Cross, with arms outstretched, he mimics the figure of Christ. Traditionally this gesture was interpreted as a declaration of the pilgrim's willingness to take up his cross and follow in the footsteps of Christ. The Station Prayer was seen as a sharing in the suffering of Christ on his way to Calvary. However it may also be the case that this gesture, made facing away from the cross and towards the east, recalls the practice of Celtic monks. They are said to have maintained this posture for hours on end as an attitude of greeting towards the rising sun, symbol of the Risen Christ.

For many pilgrims, as the Station Prayer progresses and is repeated, a sense of peace and calm develops. The physical and mental repetitions of movement and prayer preoccupy the mind and body and eliminate other distractions. It is certainly the case that even if large numbers of pilgrims are engaged in their Station Prayers, the atmosphere on the island is very quiet and peaceful. This not only assists the pilgrims in praying but also

helps create an environment for reflection which is often difficult to find amid the pressures and distractions of the world of
everyday life.

For many people, Lough Derg provides an opportunity to
step back from their lives, to take stock and to examine the direction which their lives are taking. Combined with the prayers and
penance of the pilgrimage, this kind of reflection forms part of
the process of conversion which lies at the heart of the pilgrimage itself.

Pilgrimage of Repentance
From its earliest origins, the pilgrimage to Lough Derg has been
a pilgrimage of repentance for the forgiveness of sin. Even during
the period when other-worldly visions dominated the general
perception of Lough Derg, all accounts agree that the primary
purpose of the pilgrimage was to atone for sin. In the modern
world the need for conversion and reconciliation, both individual and communal, remains as strong as ever. On Lough Derg,
the pilgrim can express that need in a concrete way and be
helped to further the process of conversion in his own life.

This emphasis on conversion and reconciliation is highlighted
in the ritual action of the pilgrimage. At its heart lies the celebration of the sacrament of reconciliation. The confession of sins
and reception of absolution has been an indispensable element
of the pilgrimage since at least the time of the Knight Owein. For
many pilgrims up to the present day, Lough Derg has been the
favoured destination when troubled with great burdens of conscience. Even as long ago as the early nineteenth century we are
told that the hearing of confessions was a major part of the
duties of the priests on the island. Bishop James Murphy of
Clogher reported in 1814 that six or seven priests were often
occupied in the confessionals for twelve hours or more every
day during the busiest part of the season.

In the early centuries of the pilgrimage, the confession of sins
followed immediately after the release of the pilgrim from the
cave. The night of vigil constituted a time of preparation for this
moment. The same is largely true of the pilgrimage today. The

Cardinal Logue visits the island in 1913

sacrament of reconciliation is celebrated in the morning after the all-night vigil. It therefore takes its place as a pivotal point in the dynamic of the pilgrimage. What is clear is that reconciliation is not something which happens in a single moment, but a process in which confession and absolution form a turning point.

From the very beginning of the pilgrimage, the process of reconciliation is in operation. The pilgrim setting out on his journey is turning once more to God, responding to the call to be converted and at peace with God and neighbour. The confession of sins is simply the admission of what needs to change in a person's life if he is truly to live up to the great commandment to love God and his neighbour. The preparation for that moment itself involves an experience of the grace of the sacrament, which helps the pilgrim to reflect honestly on his life and accept the need for change. During the pilgrimage there is time and space to do this.

The pilgrimage also provides the opportunity to begin the most difficult phase in the process of reconciliation. The conclusion of the pilgrimage involves returning to the life which the pilgrim has briefly left behind. If the experience of pilgrimage has changed the pilgrim, then that life too should be changed, as the process of reconciliation continues. Ó hUiginn's poetic image of Lough Derg as a tranquil place of healing remains a potent analogy of the pilgrimage experience. The island sanctuary can still be a sacred place for the healing of memories, where the pilgrim finds a remedy for the soul's ills and the possibility of spiritual regeneration.

Baptismal Imagery

The marked baptismal symbolism of the pilgrimage reinforces the central theme of conversion. In the early centuries of Christianity, the reconciliation of penitents with God and the Christian community was sometimes described as a second baptism. On Lough Derg, the transformation of the Christian through baptism is recalled in words and gestures which emphasise that it is conversion and reconciliation that bring the Christian to the fulfilment of the sacrament. We have already discussed the symbolic rituals of cleansing with water which were a feature of the pilgrimage in times gone by. The vestiges of these rituals persist in the saying of prayers at the water's edge. The Christian baptismal promises are recalled in the triple renunciation of the world, the flesh and the devil by the pilgrim at Saint Brigid's Cross.

The baptismal imagery of the night vigil is perhaps less clear. This was much more apparent when the vigil took place in the cave. The incarceration of the pilgrim in the cave for twenty-four hours, and his release, parallel the entombment of Christ. Baptism has traditionally been seen as the process by which a human being dies and rises with Christ. Death to sin and resurrection to new life is at the heart of our understanding of the sacrament. The rituals surrounding the cave on Station Island were powerfully symbolic of this process, even to the point of a Requiem Mass being said for the pilgrims before entering the cave. Today the closing of the doors of the Bascilia at the beginning of the night vigil is about all that remains of the old ritual, but the night of prayer is still reminiscent of the darkness of Christ's tomb and the expectation of the light of resurrection.

The baptismal aspect of the pilgrimage has been made more explicit in recent years by the introduction on the second day of a short ceremony involving the renewal of baptismal promises and sprinkling with water. This ritual takes place not long after the celebration of the sacrament of reconciliation and links the two sacraments together as sources of renewal in the Christian life.

The Mass

The renewal of the liturgy is also apparent in the celebration of the eucharist on Lough Derg. The Mass has always been an essential element of the pilgrimage. We have seen how the saying of a Requiem Mass preceded entry into the cave. This practice probably disappeared when the cave was finally closed. From the early nineteenth century the emphasis was on the worthy reception of Holy Communion at Mass. To this end the penitential exercises, sermons and finally confession were seen as the essential preparation. Nowadays the emphasis has shifted towards the celebration of the eucharist as the sacrifice of praise and thanksgiving offered by God's people. The celebration of Mass on Lough Derg has a character and atmosphere which is in some ways unique and quite memorable. It is almost certainly the case that the process of bonding between pilgrims which we have already mentioned has the effect of creating a sense of unity in the worshipping assembly. The impression of active participation is apparent not only in the more obvious aspects such as singing, but also in the moments of silence and contemplation. There is truly a sense of being in the presence of a united body of Christ and of witnessing an expression of the power of reconciliation. For if the sacrament of reconciliation has as its goal the overcoming of division between God and his people, then the eucharist is the sacrament which expresses and strengthens that unity.

The Twenty-First Century

It may well be that at some future time the advent of the new millennium will be seen as also marking a turning point in the history of Lough Derg. Certainly at this point in time it appears that some of the old certainties and traditions of the pilgrimage have waned. But in their place there is perhaps an increasing vitality, a greater sense of the richness of the experience which the pilgrimage has to offer. The work that has been done in the last decades of the twentieth century in renewing not just the fabric of the island, but more importantly the liturgical spirit of the pilgrimage, has contributed greatly to opening up the Lough Derg experience to new generations of pilgrims. It is heartening to think that in a new millennium and a changing world, an ancient pilgrimage can preserve the best of past ages whilst responding to the needs of present and future Christians.

Fare thee well, Lough Derg

The Priors of Lough Derg

490	St Dabheoc (the elder)
820	Abbot Patrick

1130-1632

Canons Regular of St Augustine
including Rev Matthew Magrath, Rev Raymond
Maguire, and Rev Turlough Maguire.

1632-1780

Franciscans
including Rev Thaddeus O'Clery, Rev MacGrath,
and Rev Anthony O'Doherty.

1780-Present day

Clergy from the Diocese of Clogher, appointed by
the Bishop of Clogher:

1780-1800	Rev Murray
1800-1829	Rev Patrick Bellew
1830	Rev Daniel Boylan
1831-1856	Rev Patrick Moynagh
1857-1876	Rev Edward McKenna
1877-1903	Rev James McKenna
1904-1908	Rev Canon Smyth
1909-1941	Monsignor Patrick Keown

parish Priest of Carrickmacross and Dean of the
Diocese of Clogher. Died 18 October 1946.

1942-1960   Monsignor Edward Cornelius Ward
Parish Priest of Latton, Co Managhan. Parish
Priest of Clones until from 1961 until 1973. Died 6
October 1973. Buried in Clones.

1961-1978   Monsignor Thomas Flood
Parish Priest of Dromore, Co Tyrone, from 1961
until 1987. Died 29 January 1987.
Buried in Dromore.

1979   Canon Sean McNaboe
A native of Dromore, Co Tyrone. Parish Priest of
Clones, Co Monaghan. Died 23 January 2000.
Buried in Clones.

1980-1990   Monsignor Gerard McSorley
A native of Newtownsaville, Co Tyrone. Became
Administrator of Pettigo Parish when appointed
Prior. Parish Priest of Ballybay, Co Monaghan,
since 1990.

1991-   Monsignor Richard Mohan
A native of Coonian, Co Fermanagh.
Administrator of the Parish of Pettigo.

Annual Numbers on Pilgrimage

*The figures for the years 1861-1913 were extracted from the notes of
the late James Canon Mc Kenna, PP,
by Rev P Keown, 29 August 1913.*

1861 - 3,816	1892 - 2,874
1862 - 2,928	1893 - 3,050
1863 - 2,634	1894 - 2,914
1864 - 2,764	1895 - 3,116
1865 - 2,352	1896 - 3,098
1866 - 3,336	1897 - 3,333
1867 - 2,533	1898 - 3,247
1868 - 2,331	1899 - 3,248
1869 - 2,387	1900 - 3,456
1870 - 2,831	1901 - 3,304
1871 - 3,293	1902 - 3,884
1872 - 3,656	1903 - 4,263
1873 - 2,992	1904 - *
1874 - 2,411	1905 - *
1875 - 2,110	1906 - *
1876 - 3,191	1907 - *
1877 - 3,294	1908 - 5,414
1878 - 3,224	1909 - S,807
1879 - 1,765	1910 - 6,012
1880 - 2,488	1911 - 6,222
1881 - 2,222	1912 - 6,147
1882 - 3,097	1913 - 6,954
1883 - 2,813	1914 - 7,170
1884 - 3,188	1915 - 9,216
1885 - 2,444	1916 - 10,584
1886 - 2,016	1917 - 10,044
1887 - 2,742	1918 - 12,420
1888 - 2,852	1919 - 14,287
1889 - 3,068	1920 - 12,004
1890 - 3,124	1921 - 8,324
1891 - 2,944	* no figures recorded

1922 - 1,308
1923 - 6,000
1924 - 6,212
1925 - 6,607
1926 - 7,563
1927 - 8,426
1928 - 9,274
1929 - 10,378
1930 - 11,800
1931 - 13,184
1932 - 12,316
1933 - 14,815
1934 - 13,947
1935 - 13,706
1936 - 12,877
1937 - 12,671
1938 - 12,102
1939 - 13,150
1940 - 13,846
1941 - 14,432
1942 - 14,742
1943 - 16,746
1944 - 19,049
1945 - 21,883
1946 - 23,564
1947 - 23,105
1948 - 24,695
1949 - 25,024
1950 - 30,963
1951 - 32,554
1952 - 34,645
1953 - 33,269
1954 - 34,039
1955 - 31,824
1956 - 28,649
1957 - 30,369
1958 - 25,044
1959 - 27,088
1960 - 25,878

1961 - 28,175
1962 - 24,337
1963 - 22,400
1964 - 22,381
1965 - 20,842
1966 - 19,921
1967 - 20,071
1968 - 19,081
1969 - 18,054
1970 - 18,048
1971 - 19,060
1972 - 17,210
1973 - 16,421
1974 - 16,692
1975 - 20,751
1976 - 19,961
1977 - 20,431
1978 - 19,799
1979 - 18,884
1980 - 21,559
1981 - 21,457
1982 - 24,330
1983 - 26,443
1984 - 29,172
1985 - 28,044
1986 - 27,622
1987 - 28,741
1988 - 28,216
1989 - 27,661
1990 - 25,390
1991 - 24,863
1992 - 22,122
1993 - 18,615
1994 - 15,813
1995 - 13,779
1996 - 12,382
1997 - 11,771
1998 - 10,973
1999 - 10,134

APPENDIX III

Annual Numbers on One-Day Retreats

1992 - approx 4000   (8 days)

1993 - 9,429   (21 days)

1994 - 11,427   (27 days)

1995 - 14,784   (20 days in May, 17 days in September)

1996 - 12,182   (22 days in May, 19 days in September)

1997 - 10,719   (20 days in May, 15 days in September)

1998 - 10,510   (20 days in May, 17 days in September)

1999 - 10,262   (19 days in May, 15 days in September)